# THE
# BEAUTY
# OF TIME

**Other Schiffer Books on Related Subjects:**
*A. Lange & Söhne® Highlights*, ISBN: 978-0-7643-4361-2
*Legendary Wristwatches*, ISBN: 978-0-7643-4957-7

Cover design by Molly Shields
Type set in Helvetica Neue

ISBN: 978-0-7643-4956-0
Printed in China

Published by Schiffer Publishing, Ltd.
4880 Lower Valley Road
Atglen, PA 19310
Phone: (610) 593-1777; Fax: (610) 593-2002
E-mail: Info@schifferbooks.com

For our complete selection of fine books on this and related subjects, please visit our website at www.schifferbooks.com. You may also write for a free catalog.

This book may be purchased from the publisher. Please try your bookstore first.

We are always looking for people to write books on new and related subjects. If you have an idea for a book, please contact us at proposals@schifferbooks.com.

Schiffer Publishing's titles are available at special discounts for bulk purchases for sales promotions or premiums. Special editions, including personalized covers, corporate imprints, and excerpts can be created in large quantities for special needs. For more information, contact the publisher.

Translated from the German by Jonee Tiedemann

Originally published as Die Schonheit Der Zeit Die Uhren Von A. Lange & Sohne by Delius Klasing, Bielefeld, © 2012 Delius Klasing

# THE

Harry Niemann

# BEAUTY

THE WATCHES OF A. LANGE & SÖHNE

# OF TIME

4880 Lower Valley Road • Atglen, PA 19310

The inclusion of press texts in this book was expressely authorized by LANGE UHREN GMBH, Glashütte.

Images were kindly provided by A. Lange & Sons, as well as by Dr. Crott Auction House (pages 21, 22, 23, 24, 25, 26, 29, and 31).

# Contents

# Impressions and Memories Instead of a Preface

When I visited a prestigious jewelry shop in the mid-'90s in Darmstadt together with my wife—a place where I had purchased one or the other mechanical watch—the general manager showed us the first collection of Lange watches of the modern era. The Lange1, the Saxonia, the Arkade, and the Tourbillon "Pour le Merité" were watches that not only featured their very own formal look and large date, but they also had extraordinary machining. They were actually small works of art—like the play of blue, red, and gold resulting from the blueing of screws and the gold chatons, the Glashütte ribbing with the golden engraving, and the three-quarter plate from natural nickel silver created an aesthetic appeal I had not seen before on any watch.

A more in-depth look revealed a hand-engraved balance cock. The construction of these watches has been raised to an artistic level that greatly surpasses mere technical requirements and turns each watch into a gem. This reinterpretation of

the Lange-style watchmaking tradition fascinated me from the very beginning.

Finally, Mr. Reisdorf looked me straight in the eye and said: "You too will one day wear a Lange watch." Apparently my wife was so impressed that she fulfilled this dream on my fiftieth birthday. Since then I have owned one of these treasures and every day I enjoy this highest expression of German watchmaking.

Later, when my publisher asked me whether I could write a book about the watches of A. Lange & Sons, I was excited; as a fan of mechanical watches, but more so since as a former in-house historian of Mercedes-Benz I had the opportunity to meet Walter Lange and his beautiful W 111 cabriolet at the Salzburg Classic Days that he hosted.

Back then I had written an article about the Mercedes fan Walter Lange in *Classic Magazin* by Mercedes-Benz, but also about Glashütte and the Lange watches, so I was somewhat familiar with the topic. When I told Walter Lange about my plan to write a small book about the watches and company A. Lange & Sons he spontaneously agreed to write the preface.

In the summer of 2010, I accompanied my wife to a health retreat in Hofgastein and intended to finish the manuscript while there. Every day from 6 a.m. on I sat at my computer and wrote. However, work should rest on Sundays, so I put on my Lange watch and went on a wonderful outing with my wife along the almost empty high pass route of the Grossglockner, up to the Kaiser-Franz-Josefs-Höhe, and then towards Heiligenblut, where we visited the pilgrimage church and its enchanted cemetery.

On the way back I noticed that I had forgotten to buy the *Frankfurter Allgemeine Sonntagszeitung* newspaper, in which I was expected to see one of my articles. It was not available at our hotel, so I went on my way to a kiosk, which was closed late in the afternoon. I then went to the nearest hotel and asked for it: sorry, apparently not—if there is no copy lying on the newspaper table then some of the guests must have taken the paper to their rooms.

I gave up and started to return when I saw a smoky, silver-colored Mercedes-Benz CLS on the right side of the street with the remarkable plate PF-MB 219. MB for Mercedes-Benz, yes! But for someone to put the internal numbering code for this series on the license plates is unusual, so I looked inside: beige leather, chestnut wood, and a pair of car gloves on the center console. I faltered, reached for my cell phone, and dialed. "Lange here." "Hello Mr. Lange, this is Niemann, just a quick question: are you in Pforzheim?" A short hesitation. "No, I am in Austria." "Yes, in Bad Hofgastein," I replied, "and I am standing next to your car, which I know so well because I was present when you picked it up in Sindelfingen." Silence at the other end of the line, then: "... I will be down right away and open the door for you."

In this manner we then sat together that Sunday, talking about watches and cars, and I was happy to take advantage of the opportunity to compose the preface.

# Preface by Company Founder Walter Lange

Until the forced collectivization of East German watchmaking after WWII, the Saxon watch manufacturer in Glashütte founded by my great grandfather, Ferdinand Adolph Lange, in the mid-nineteenth century had been creating precision pocket watches that were among the most prestigious and coveted watches in the world. For over forty years the name A. Lange & Söhne disappeared; today, looking back, I am still amazed that I managed to revive this traditional company—together with Günter Blümlein (1943-2001)—right after the German reunification, and once again made A. Lange & Sons one of the leading international watch brands. Today, when I walk through the rooms of our former family company where there is busy activity, I sense a deep gratitude and joy. The quality of the products and the enthusiasm of the staff have raised the brand from the ashes like a phoenix and it shines more brilliantly than ever. It is the genius loci that makes it possible. Lange is part of the historic Saxon legacy, and the new company has brought time to Glashütte for a second period. During the past twenty years there have been numerous publications about our watches and the topic of Lange; however, I am confident that this author will present the products and history of our company in this book in a compact and well-written manner and provide a good decision-making tool for all those who would like to wear a A. Lange & Söhne on their wrist. I wish the reader much enjoyment while reading, as well as while looking at the watches and watch movements, which are all small works of art that you can enjoy anew every day.

Walter Lange

# History of Watchmaking in Glashütte and the Rise of A. Lange & Söhne

The watchmaking heritage and family line of the Langes is deeply rooted in the most splendid period of Saxony. It actually started when a certain Christian Gutkaes (1682–1757), together with the French gourmet cooks Joseph Le Bon and Jean L'Enfant, served the Saxon sovereign August the Strong as Royal Saxon court cooks, who took the throne in Dresden over 300 years ago, in 1694. Friedrich August I (born May 12, 1670, in Dresden, died February 1, 1733, in Warsaw)—Elector of Saxony and often called August the Strong—came from the Wettin line. He was the second-oldest son of Johann Georg I of Saxony and princess Anna Sophie of Denmark and Norway. From 1697 on, as August II he was also King of Poland and Grand Duke of Lithuania. To make this possible he secretly converted to Catholicism. However, the Polish crown came at a high price for the Saxons: thirty-nine million Reichstaler in bribe money went to the Polish aristocracy to get their consent. On the other hand, it was August the Strong who, due to his pronounced self-portrayal that found expression in architecture and art, made Dresden a metropolis of the Baroque. This was accompanied by an enormous economic and cultural golden period.

He significantly shaped Saxony as an admirer of the sciences and arts, wordly architecture, and as a lover of beautiful women. August the Strong was also one of the most important watch collectors. He accumulated a collection of the most beautiful timekeepers of these times that can still be admired at the Mathematical-Physical Salon of the Zwinger. This collection was later curated by court clock-maker Johann Friedrich Schumann, the great-great-great-grandfather of Walter Lange. Schumann's daughter married watchmaker Johann Christian Friedrich Gutkaes in 1815.

Gutkaes became a mechanicus-watchmaker, at first at the Mathematical-Physical Salon and then, in 1842, he became a court watchmaker. The creator of the famous five-minute watch for the

Johann Christian Friedrich Gutkaes, teacher and father-in-law of Ferdinand Adolph Lange.

Ferdinand Adolph Lange, 1815–1875.

first Semper opera in Dresden was the teacher and later father-in-law of Ferdinand Adolph Lange, the great-grandfather of Walter Lange. The history of Ferdinand Adolph Lange is about watches and about people: those whose creations were world famous and those whom he taught his skills as a gifted teacher. Almost no other life achievement is so thoroughly documented as that of Adolph Lange. This is due to the extraordinary watches bearing his or his family's name. However, the son of gunsmith Samuel Lange born February 18, 1815, in Dresden was not gifted with such a career. Soon the mother divorced the father, who was known as a "man with a rough character." Another family took care of the intelligent but frail Adolph Lange, promoted him, and found him an apprenticeship with the already prestigious court clockmaker Johann Christian Friedrich Gutkaes. The foreman quickly recognized not only the boy's exceptional manual dexterity, but also his unusual ambition to go further than was common for a watchmaker in Dresden at that time. Lange did his apprenticeship, visited the recently established polytechnical school, and stud-

Pocket chronometer movement by A. Lange & Söhne
with impulse via fusee and chain, around 1868.

ied English and French at night. His plan was formed early on: all he wanted to do was increase his knowledge at the centers for highly developed watchmaking in France and England. The creative watchmaking craft that originated during the Renaissance in German-speaking areas—Nurnberg, Augsburg, Schaffhausen, and Strasbourg—had migrated to London and Paris. In the glamorous environment of courtly life and while searching for ever-more precise timekeepers for military and civilian seafaring, watchmaking received continuous and lasting state support.

In 1837—three years after his apprenticeship in Dresden—Adolph Lange packed his bags, had his foreman Meister Gutkaes write a recommendation in his sketchbook, and began his service for the famous watchmaker Joseph Thaddäus Winnerl in Paris. The latter had been one of the best students of Abraham Louis Brequet. In short, a study trip turned into three years, during which Lange rose up to become the shop manager. In the end, he had to decline Winnerl's offer to stay, as his travel plans still included England and Switzerland. During these times his

Ferdinand Adolph Lange's first workshop in Glashütte.

famous sketchbook filled up with clock movement, detailed drawings, and mathematical calculations for wheels and pinions. Lange's tables were based on the metric system, which was introduced at the same time by Antoine LeCoultre in Le Sentier. Adolph Lange was not a fan of the trial and error that dominated horology in those days and made it impossible to achieve a consistent, reproducible quality.

With the firm intent to change this, he returned to Gutkaes's watchmaking manufacture, married his daughter Charlotte Amalie Antonia in 1842, and became a partner and watchmaking "engine" at the workshop of his father-in-law. This shop produced famous precision regulators for the observatories of several countries. One of them—with number 32—is located at the Geneva Musée d'Histoire des Sciences and provided the exact time for the country of watches from a Swiss observatory for some sixty years. Apart from his adoption of the metric system and hence new possible quality norms, Lange brought another decisive insight home with him from England and Switzerland. It is recorded in a letter directed in January 1844 to the

Saxony Privy Government Council von Weissenbach, where he asked for support for his project in Glashütte:

> With the pleasing shape of the Swiss cylinder watch I unite the long duration and already recognized precision of the very expensive yet unwieldy English anchor watch.

The legendary Glashütte anchor movement would eventually be his trademark. This also revealed his work ethic and principle: he was always improving things and he was a perfectionist. Ferdinand Adolph Lange was one of the first to apply the metric system, replacing the complicated and then-valid Parisian measurement.

Adolph Lange's sketchbook provides proof of this. It was also the intellectual foundation for the creation of the Lange Uhren GmbH in December 1990. However, Adolph Lange was not only a gifted watchmaker and an educated and very religious man; he also had a social conscience. The bitter conditions in structurally weak Erzgebirge that the government was unable to manage caused him to act in 1844. He promoted his project in letters, petitions, and conversations until the contract with the Royal Saxon Interior Ministry in Dresden came to fruition and he built a watch manufacturing plant in Glashütte. Lange committed to train fifteen teenagers from Glashütte to become watchmakers within three years, while the state would provide a repayable credit of 6,700 thaler and another 1,120 thaler for the acquisition of tools. The apprentices were to work for another five years at Lange's shop and pay back the cost of their apprenticeship with weekly payments of twenty-four Neugroschen. As future watchmakers, Adolph Lange saw "1 painting assistant, 12 straw weavers, 4 domestic servants, 1 farm hand, 1 quarry, and 1 wine grower," as shown by the first list of employees. Although he had to let some of these "nature boys" go after a brief probation period due to lacking aptitude, the rest of them persevered and formed the core of his team, which he quickly expanded to thirty young professionals.

In the beginning Lange had hardly any qualified personnel, except for his brother-in-law. Glashütte was an impoverished hamlet with a town charter since 1506 that had long since left behind its heyday as a mining town; silver-containing glass ore discoveries were connected to a world with a once-per-week stagecoach and a barely driveable road. When the illiterate coachman emptied the post bag, everybody had to pick his own correspondence from the pile. Other than that, ponds with geese and manure heaps characterized the town's scenery.

F. ADOLPH LANGE.

Lange fitted out the workshop, taught his apprentices, and built up a first line of production while simultaneously building better machines for making precision parts; he also managed correspondence and took care of accounting. His daughter Emma reported occasional collapses of her father who was working until late at night, who had put all of his assets, including those of his wife and even the prize money he received from watchmaking awards into the continuously threatened startup.

However, his visionary concept took shape: apart from his own company, Glashütte—whose infrastructure Adolph Lange had greatly improved as its mayor for eighteen years—saw the establishment of many small specialty workshops for the manufacture of stones, screws, wheels and discs, barrels, balances, and hands. Casemakers, gilders, guillocheurs, and three additional manufacturing shops—some of which worked for him—were created due to his sponsorship and were often founded by people who had earlier served an apprenticeship. Hundreds of secure and

Monument dedicated to Ferdinand Adolph Lange, built in 1895 in Glashütte.

16

well-paid jobs converted destitution into humble prosperity.

Lange's staff rarely surpassed 100 employees, and it remained the core of German fine watchmaking prospering in and around Glashütte. Lange was unique, in that he wanted to market absolutely perfectly timed pocket watches that did not require re-machining, so the heretofore common finishing or "repassage"—the disassembly and reworking of a watch by a manufacturer, including the "reglage"—did not apply. Lange realized that with construction of the movement and precise workmanship adjustability could be decisively influenced.

The watchmaking school "Deutsche Uhrmacherschule" (DUS) that he initiated in 1878 with his theoretically-inclined friend Moritz Grossmann ("Der freie Ankergang" - "The free anchor escapement") definitely cut off the umbilical cord of Glashütte regarding the practical and theoretical training of its staff in Switzerland and France and cemented its reputation as the German center of fine watchmaking. When Adolph Lange unexpectedly passed away on December 3, 1875, at sixty-one, he not only left his sons and grandchildren a thriving company and a series of international awards, but the region of

17

In 1902, Emil Lange received the Knight's Cross of the French Legion.

Glashütte now had a secure economic future. The city built a memorial for him. Adolph Lange had brought back fine watchmaking to Germany and re-formed it from the ground up. His designs with the first precisely calculated components, a new structural base with a three-quarter plate, the custom Glashütte-style anchor escapement and compensation balance, and fine regulation or spirals with special end curves represent the highest standard of watchmaking. The precision watches of A. Lange & Sons—among them highly complicated pieces that command top prices at auctions today—preserve the philosophy of a man who has co-written the history of watches, as well as a part of the Saxon industrial history for fans of mechanical timekeeping. The watches signed "A. Lange & Sons" from Glashütte carry this high prestige into the future.

Richard Lange (born December 17, 1845, in Dresden; died October 29, 1932, in Oberlöschnitz-Radebeul) continued the company with his brother Emil Lange (born August 30, 1849, in Glashütte; died October 9, 1922, in Blasewitz, Dresden). Richard Lange was a watchmaker who was trained by his father in practical knowledge and by Moritz Grossmann in theoretical knowledge. Emil Lange was in charge of business. When his brother retired from management in 1886, he took over and continued for forty-six years. In

1909, his son Otto Lange (November 4, 1878—January 29, 1971) joined the company and, together with Rudolf Lange (March 22, 1884—August 7, 1954), took over its management. Rudolf's son, Walter Lange, also a master watchmaker, could not continue the operation of the company; however, after the reunification in 1990 he would successfully complete a large coup.

# Historical Pocket- and Wristwatches by A. Lange & Söhne

This book presents mostly products of the new era, that is, wristwatches manufactured in Glashütte since 1994 with the label "A. Lange & Sons." However, looking back at those products that set the standard for modern watches is of interest to Lange enthusiasts. Moreover, every friend of Lange wristwatches will one day think about how nice it might be to have a vintage pocketwatch by this very company in their casket. Pocketwatches by A. Lange & Sons are among today's sought-after collector items.

The really valuable ones are in the famous 1A-quality range. What does this mean? For one, they can be recognized by the engraving "A. Lange & Söhne, Glashütte bei Dresden." The watch features screwed gilded chatons at all of the visible pivot bearings on the plate, including the anchor cock and the diamond endstone. The movements are gilded; those destined for export are nickel-plated. To reduce the influence of magnetism and to optimize the center of mass of the anchor plate

and anchor, these pieces are made from 8-carat hammered gold. Up until 1933, 1A-quality cases consisted of 18-carat gold. On the dial of these so-called ALS-branded watches one will notice the semicircular "A. Lange & Söhne" and below it "Glashütte -SA." Collectors also speak of 1B- and 1C-quality watches, but these never officially existed. From 1906 on, Lange launched a sort of second brand called DUF to hold ground against local competition (created by the foundation of the "Glashütter Präzisionsuhren Akt. Ges" in 1904) and international competition. The DUF brand also features a 3/4 plate with the semicircular dial inscription "Deutsche Uhrenfabrikation" and below it "Glashütte-SA. A. Lange & Söhne." These watches were also hand-made, but they were a more simple edition without screwed chatons and gold screws. Rather than the five layers of 1A-quality, the DUF watches featured only three layers. All versions feature extraordinarily fine case craftsmanship. The rather common rupture of the case

A unique early Glashütte Savonnette with a second time zone, with precise adjustment via an hour and minutes ring made in 1A quality. The weight is 123 grams (4.3 ounces) and it has a 52 mm diameter. Built around 1878.

spring was avoided by Lange with his patented "Wurffeder" ("throw spring"). The cases were made at Lange by an independent division that worked of its own accord and was justifiably self-confident.

Due to constant technological improvements the age of a Lange watch can be precisely dated by an expert. With pride they point out that the highly-developed machining technology is exclusively used for the precise manufacture of various pieces, however, it is not utilized to make "template watches" during mass fabrication in Switzerland. One must and wants to differentiate oneself, and hence one can read in the catalog: "Our apparently high prices, when considering the special inner value of our watches while looking at them

An important and extremely rare Glashütte Savonnette with split-seconds hand chronograph—chronograph rattrapante. In the 100-year history of A. Lange & Söhne, only thirty-five units of this highly complicated watch were built. The weight is 156 grams (5.5 ounces), 52 mm diameter. Built in 1894.

An outstanding and unique Glashütte Savonnette with chronograph and a black dial. This is the only pocket watch by Lange & Söhne with a black dial. The weight is 121 grams (4.26 ounces), 54 mm diameter. Built around 1908.

in detail, is not only extremely advantageous and appropriate, but also economical, as the utilization of only the best and most durable materials and our many years of experience with excellent machining methods raise the lifespan of our watches in such a way that, when built together with only the most solid cases, they are still dependable timepieces after forty to fifty years and always present a dignified and elegant look."

In the catalogs, the brands ALS and DUF coexist peacefully. Thus, the three-hand watches with a small second on the six are offered as the "Jürgens" or "Lucia" models with a silver or gold case in sizes between 41 and 45 mm. The former is also available as a 47-mm anchor chronometer but only as an ALS, again in silver or 18-carat gold. The price of a watch is determined by the material, case size and brand, and whether it is a Lépine or Savonnette. For example, a DUF model "Jürgens" weighing about 35 grams in 14-carat gold with a 43-mm diameter as a Lépine commands between 289 and 309

Glashütte Savonnette with alarm clock; only six of them were built. Sold in 1919 for 3,776 marks ($2,110) and manufactured in 1A quality. The 18-carat gold case is shaped as "royal a goutte." The weight is 132 grams (4.65 ounces), 54 mm diameter. Built around 1919.

marks ($162-174). In the case of a Savonnette it would be 340 to 365 marks ($191-205). In comparison, an ALS with a 43-mm case diameter in 18-carat gold weighing about 40 grams costs between 409 to 438 ($230-246) for the Lépine and 486 to 520 marks ($273-292) for the Savonnette. In the case of this model, which is also fitted as an anchor chronometer with an extra large balance and a 47-mm case diameter, the Savonnette costs between 724 and 775 marks ($407-436), or twice as much as the DUF model.

The different prices result from the extras that can be ordered with the watch, such as golden pear hands, glass over the movement, gold cuvette on the inside, and gold or silver crown and rubies in the movement itself, sometimes with a gold bushing. An anchor chronometer as a model "Lucia 9 Pommes" with a 47-mm case diameter could cost up to 858 marks ($483) during peacetime. Next to simple silver cases, those made from Tula silver with different patterns such as chain, line, or wood were offered as well. Gold watches

Rare Glashütte Savonnette with automatic winding, power reserve indicator, anti-magnetic version. This is the only automatic pocket watch by Lange & Söhne with a power reserve indicator at the one. The weight is 192 grams (6.77 ounces), 60 mm diameter.

offered monograms or coat of arms engravings for a surcharge, as well as enamel and gemstone decoration.

At the beginning of the twentieth century more men's models were available, including the "Imperial" and "Royal," "Louis XV" and "Louis XVI," "Breguet," and "Cavalier a goutte." While the former models were available both as ALS and DUF, the latter were only available as DUF or, in the case of the former, as ALS. Furthermore, there were all kinds of complications available, including the Grosse Komplikation ("Big Complication"), featuring a self-striking minutes repeater, a double chronograph with rattrapante and minutes counter, and a perpetual calendar. The Chronograph and the Chronograph Rattrapante were also available. There was even an automatic pocket watch model with the reserve wind-up mechanism in the program—together with a tourbillon carousel and a deadbeat seconds recommended for medical doctors—while the simple chronographs and the "Seconde Morte" were available as a DUF version.

Glashütte Savonnette in an early anti-magnetic version with minutes repetition and split-seconds hand with 30-minute counter, sold on May 30, 1901, to the Hinselmann company in Essen for 2,504 marks ($1,400) and manufactured in 1A quality. The weight is 186 grams (6.56 ounces), 60 mm diameter. Built in 1901.

More surprising still is that the complications such as quarter repetition, minute repetition, and the same with additional chronograph were also available in the DUF brand. Only the Grosse Komplikation ("Large Complication") was—just like the double chronograph—only available as an ALS; that is, in 1A quality. The most expensive minute repetition with chronograph cost 4,190 marks ($2,358). The normal Chronograph was priced at 1,110 marks ($624) and the Double Chronograph at 1,553 marks ($874). For comparison, in 1905, the top model of Benz & Cie. in Mannheim, the Benz 35/40 PS-cardan coach—as a limousine or even as a landaulet—cost 25,000 marks ($14,072). A worker in those times made about 1,500 marks ($844) a year. A "Grande Complication" with a self-striking mechanism and large and small chime, a minutes repetition, a split-seconds hand (slave pointer) with minute counter and blinking second, a perpetual calendar, and a moon phase

Kaiser Wilhelm II. gave this A. Lange &
Söhne pocket watch to sultan Abdul
Hamid II during his visit to Turkey in 1898.
Today the watch is owned by the Topkapi
Sarayi Museum in Istanbul.

indicator was available via ALS for 5,600 marks ($3,152). Then as now, it was not exactly a cheap matter to call an A. Lange & Sons watch your own.

Another affordable brand was produced between 1919 and 1925. The name OLIW (Original Lange International Works) indicates the watch contains a bridge movement with a pallet stone escapement instead of the Glashütte anchor escapement. Hence, from the standpoint of the collector it is rather trivial, even if the dial says among other things "Langeuhr" ("Lange watch"). In retrospect, Lange also missed the development of a high-quality wristwatch clockwork movement.

To still be able to deliver the sought-after wristwatch from the 1930s on Lange bought in Switzerland. Lange used movements by the company Altus and the dial says "A. Lange & Söhne Genf." Only with the Kaliber 48—whose name derived from its 48-mm diameter—was a movement for marine chronometers built that was appropriate for wristwatches. Today—with overly large wristwatches in the fried-egg format—such a historic Lange watch is nice to wear. While Lange watches with Altus movements are not much sought after, the case is entirely different for the Kaliber 48.

Watches of the ALS and DUF brands were very much sought after and promoted quite a lot. The catalog for the two core brands announces: "The good reputation of Lange precision watches is based on several factors: 1. the utilized materials undergo a special increase in quality due to the machining methods derived from experience; 2. the highly developed machining technology is only utilized for the precise manufacture of individual components, not for mass fabrication and to lower costs (no template watches); 3. only staff which have been trained for many years and specialized according to their inclinations to work a particular part or its function are employed; 4. The manufactured movements which are made utilizing modern technologies, combined with excellent craftsmanship, are checked as to all of their parts in minute detail by select experts. Custom-made measuring instruments are utilized which can detect inaccuracies of 1/100 to 1/1000 of a millimeter or a gram; 5. A continuous supervision of all of the watches is performed by the manager of the company so that the sense of responsibility of each staff member is encouraged to the highest degree until finally a special check of the finished watch is performed by the manager."

The company trained watchmakers and representatives, enabling them to explain the advantages and features of a Lange watch to interested clients. This included a corresponding presence in printed media. Lange delivered any

Glashütte Savonnette "Grande Complication" with double chronograph, perpetual calendar, moon phase, and minutes repetition —formerly with rate register of the University Observatory of Leipzig —sold on November 25, 1898, for 3,000 marks ($1,676). Manufactured in 1A quality. The weight is 210 grams (7.4 ounces), 60 mm diameter. Built in 1898.

imaginable watch case for a corresponding payment: "Silver, gold, even platinum, the most noble materials protect and adorn the movement of a precision watch in a dignified manner. In special retailer's window displays you can see our watches with the most modern cases designed by artists that please any requirement with their numerous decorations and shapes. We also offer simple, basic, and yet perfect watch cases which, because of their harmonious dimensions, can be called classic. Independent of the current fashion, they stand tall over passing tastes and you will always receive compliments and appreciation because of their long life.

The large polished surfaces of these cases suffer only the most minimal wear and retain their elegant look even after decades of use. For almost a century our company has been delivering the most exquisite watches to its clients. All of our

Extremely rare Glashütte Savonnette with perpetual calendar, moon phase and minutes repetition. Weighing some 205 grams (7.23 ounces), this is the heaviest minutes repetition with perpetual calendar; only nine were manufactured. The 1A quality watch was sold in 1904 for 2,926 marks ($1,635). Diameter of 60 mm.

expertise and the skills of our staff go into the making of these small movements."

We also read in the publication of this advertisement: "We hope that our products will become living intermediaries between humans, that all of our diligence and accuracy that we have applied to manufacture will convert with the future wearer into satisfaction and enjoyment in owning an original Glashütte Lange watch."

Nothing can be added to this, apart from the fact that these wishes from the past should accompany the owner of a new Lange watch.

# The Genius Loci or the Rebirth of a Traditional Company

When Walter Lange's great-grandfather decided to develop a watch company in the economically depressed area of Müglitztal he could be certain to receive support from the Royal Saxon interior ministry, as Saxony had an elemental interest in providing its residents with bread and work. The considerable sum of 5,580 thaler formed the seed capital for a watch manufacture in Glashütte. The official inauguration of the plant occurred on December 7, 1845. What began with the production of high-quality yet simple pocket watches over the years developed into a production facility of haute horology. Choice pocket watches with tourbillon, perpetual calendar, chronographs, and even pocket watches with automatic winding mechanisms were sent out into the world.

After the formation of the German Reich in 1871, the imperial household was part of the client base. In the "nation that came too late," which quickly tried to catch up with England regarding industrialization, the Saxons were the keepers of exact time, which was now very much a necessity. Not only precise, but also highly complicated watches were delivered, including a Grosse Komplikation with minute repeater, 4/4 beat, perpetual calendar, and rattrapante chronograph, whose price of 4,930 goldmarks ($2,775) equaled that of a small house. Over several decades the family skillfully managed the company with commercial expertise through peacetime and times of war.

Walter Lange, born in 1924 and trained as a master watchmaker, would continue this tradition.

But then WWII broke out. On May 8, 1945, a German tank unit moved through Glashütte while retreating. Twenty-one-year-old Walter Lange, who had suffered a grave war injury and was resting for a day at the family home, was awakened early in the morning by a series of bomb explosions. Russian fighter pilots had located the German units and were attacking. However, the bombs not only hit the vehicles of the fleeing soldiers, but also the heart of

The main production building of A. Lange & Söhne in Glashütte was destroyed during a bomb raid on May 8, 1945.

Glashütte: the main production building of A. Lange & Sons went up in flames.

The destruction from the air was soon followed by the plundering of all that still appeared useful. Nevertheless, the staff still present immediately started to recover and repair damaged machines. Pieces of watches ripped from drawers that had fallen to the ground were collected and cleaned. A. Lange & Sons notified watchmaking shops all over Germany that had been assembling the Kaliber 48 for the observation watch, asking them to send still existing components back to Glashütte. There was no possibility of continuing production for the time being. The joint owners of the company were Otto, Gerhard, and Rudolf Lange (1884—1954), the latter Walter Lange's father. While the remaining watchmaking plants in Glashütte were stripped, there was nothing left to pack up at A. Lange & Sons due to bomb damage. Instead, young watchmaker Walter Lange was forced to document the entire manufacturing process of the coveted Lange Kaliber 48 as a deck watch, pilot wristwatch, and B-chronometer in writing and with drawings while under

Russian supervision. Meanwhile, clock movements were again assembled from available parts in rented rooms while the reconstruction of the destroyed plant progressed. Production was supposed to start again in May 1948. A wristwatch movement had actually been developed with the Kaliber 28 as a smaller version of the Kaliber 48.

However, the first destruction of the plant due to war was soon followed by a second—this time by a despotic political decision. Although none of the three joint owners was a member of the National Socialist organization and, even during the war, only watches had been made at A. Lange & Sons, there was an attempt to confiscate the entire holdings of the family in May 1946 based on Order no. 124, which expropriated war and Nazi criminals. This obviously unfounded decree was suspended in April 1946. However, on April 20, 1948, the government, via a new order by the occupation force, confiscated the plant and all pertinent assets. A courageous written petition by forty-five plant employees in favor of the Lange family was ineffective. Plant management was taken over by a representative of the FDGB union (Freier Deutscher Gewerkschaftsbund), which was subordinate to the SED government. Walter Lange, who at the time was working at the repair division and refused to join the FDGB, was compelled to work at a uranium

mining site and left Glashütte, heading westward. His parents continued to live at the company headquarters until they were arrested in 1953.

Only after 1976 did the GDR stop persecuting people as "fugitives of the republic" who, during the first years of the postwar period, had fled their homes or were forced to flee. Since this time Walter Lange, who had settled close to Pforzheim, visited Glashütte once a year. Meanwhile, events that took place there do not give much hope of ever reviving A. Lange & Sons: after the confiscation it was converted into the "State-Owned Enterprise A. Lange & Söhne" and later into the "Mechanik Lange & Söhne VEB." In 1951, the disowned companies A. Lange & Sons, Urofa, Ufag, and Otto Estler, as well as the mechanical precision businesses Lindig & Wolf and R. Mühle und Gössel & Co. merged to form the Glashütter Uhrenbetriebe (GUB) and the famous signet "A. Lange & Söhne" was buried in history. Walter Lange: "The name was not needed anymore and, fortunately, it was never misused, and I have always been thankful to the GUB for it." Glashütte continued to make only mechanical watches until the 1980s. Technical knowledge—despite increasing economic problems—was passed on at a high level.

This chicanery the founding family had to suffer from the "worker's and peasant's state" was not over with the expropriation of the company. When master watchmaker Walter Lange refused to join the FDBG union he was forcibly committed to work in uranium mines. Now the young man realized his stay could not last any longer if he did not want to suffer physical and mental damage. He went to Pforzheim to work for the local jewelry industry—among others the Wellendorf company—as a sales representative. There were certainly plans to once again produce his own Lange watches in the city of watches and jewelry. However, he was unsuccessful in reviving the family business in Baden-Wuerttemberg.

First contacts with the International Watch Company (IWC) in Schaffhausen led to a project of pocket watches that could not be realized due to the developing quartz crisis. However, the connections with Schaffhausen would prove valuable in the near future. The real chance for a new company foundation came about after the fall of the Berlin wall in 1989. Together with Günter Blümlein—CEO of IWC and the marketing manager of the project—the rebirth of A. Lange & Sons was put into practice. Blümlein had budgeted about a half million marks ($28,000); in the end it amounted to twenty million marks ($11,258,000).

Exactly 150 years after the company's founding, Walter Lange inscribed the company into the commercial registry on December 7, 1990. The goal was set out clearly: to once again build the world's best and most beautiful watches. Glashütte at that time was still under the spell of socialism, and the coordinates of luxury and exclusivity were rather unknown. Whoever was walking the streets back then would hardly believe the old luster would make a comeback. And still, there were many names and faces that were tightly related to the skills of A. Lange & Sons and were willing and able to cooperate with the new beginning.

Contrary to Adolph Lange in his time, who at first had to train peasant boys and simple craftsmen as watchmakers, Walter Lange was able to put together a core staff of the best Glashütte watchmakers. Walter Lange remarks about this initial period: "When we started over and re-founded the company on December 7, 1990, we basically had the famous sketch-book of my great-grandfather that was in my posession; kind of the Magna Carta for future dealings regarding the name A. Lange & Sons. We had enormous expectations of a faithful community of enthusiasts and Lange connoisseurs, but there was skepticism as well. And at first we had lots of practical problems starting our project once again. There was certainly an indispensable know-how transfer from Schaffhausen towards Glashütte during the first four years of the reconstruction. All

The headquarters of A. Lange & Söhne in Glashütte.

of the Lange employees, watchmakers, designers, engineers, and toolmakers underwent additional training in the most modern production and measurement technologies available today for watchmaking. Today, the most modern and precise numerically controlled machines are utilized in Glashütte. Not one person of the team had to start from zero."

Before the watches were presented to the public, leading concessionaires such as Wempe und Huber were invited to Glashütte to provide expert opinion regarding expected public interest.

The moment came on October 24, 1994. The Lange 1, Arkade, Saxonia, and the tourbillon "Pour le Mérite" models were presented in a large and comprehensive press campaign. The distinctive feature of the watches—the patented large date—was cleverly included with the presentation. Whenever they featured a date display, all of the dials showed the date when the reports about Saxony's new old watch

First presentation of the new collection on October 24, 1994, at the Dresden Castle with Günter Blümlein, Walter Lange, and Hartmut Knothe.

The employees of Lange Uhren GmbH in front of Lange headquarters.

brand would be published. The *Frankfurter Allgemeine Zeitung* published a two-page color ad with the following: "The economy of the East suddenly ticks in an entirely different way: A. Lange & Sons is back—the legend has once again become a watch."

When the first watches of the collection started making the rounds the tension was enormous. The reaction: overwhelming enthusiasm, likely supported by the fact that after so many years, a German luxury watch was finally competing with the large Swiss brands. To fire up the genius loci had not been easy, but the products were enchanted from the very first moment.

The watches with the three-quarter plate from nickel silver, the hand-engraved balance cock, and the wonderful color play of ruby-red bearing stones with the blued screws immediately delighted the circle of enthusiasts of mechanical watches from all over the world. Furthermore, the fact that each model series features its

own movement is another special attribute. In the end, it was due to Walter Lange, whose faith in the return of this traditional brand to its hometown made it possible. It is not surprising that the city declared him an honorary citizen in 1995 and awarded him the "Order of Merit of the Freestate of Saxony" in 1998.

Walter Lange accompanies this rapid recovery not only as a partner and brand ambassador, but particularly regarding the evaluation of the product. No watch model is produced unless it is meticulously tested. A watch can only say "A. Lange & Söhne" if the plant can back up the Lange name. But his enthusiasm is not limited to watches. *Mercedes Classic Magazin* wrote about Walter Lange and his love for automobiles with the star on the hood: "Not only is he a connoisseur of watches, but also of automobiles. His favorite vintage car is the 250 SE coupé of the W 111 production series, which was built between 1965 and 1967. Its

Walter Lange: master watchmaker and founder of Lange Uhren GmbH, born in 1924 in Glashütte.

injection engine, with an output of 150 HP, allowed for a top speed of 190 km/h [118 mph] and an acceleration from 0 to 100 km/h [62 mph] in 11.8 seconds. Driving comfort and secure road handling are provided by the single-pivot swinging axle with hydropneumatic compensating springs and automatic levelling. The lavish dashboard is made from a combination of wood and leather. The two round instruments are clearly defined: classic tachometer and revolution counter. The car, which was delivered on November 25, 1966, cost a considerable sum of 27,493 Deutschmark [$15,475]. The owner received, apart from the green leather seats, a power steering system, an electric sun roof, and a 'Becker Grand Prix' radio. Both a visual and a haptic treat is the ivory-colored steering wheel which provides a special touch to the car to this day."

Whenever his scarce time allows for it he enjoys a trip in the Mercedes vintage car." He is a most welcome guest at Mercedes-Benz during Classic Days, a meeting for enthusiasts of classic Mercedes automobiles. He is still the brand ambassador for A. Lange & Sons and its products. For him, the return to Glashütte is the fulfillment of a lifelong dream. This is also revealed by the title of his autobiography, *Als die Zeit nach Hause kam* ("When Time Came Home").

# The Traditional Values of the A. Lange & Söhne Brand and Its Contemporary Interpretation

While watch brands such as Rolex produce over a million watches per year, A. Lange & Sons produces a mere 5,500 units at the manufacturing plant located at the entrance of Glashütte. The initial modest number of 270 employees has grown to 500; half of the staff are watchmakers. To achieve distinction from the Swiss competition it is not enough to provide excellent production quality. The supply of different complications, such as chronograph, rattrapante, tourbillon, or perpetual calendar alone, or in combination, is offered by other manufacturers of luxury watches. The difference with Lange is the inner beauty of the watch. From the very beginning, the guidelines consisted of the features of traditional pocket watches. Their distinctive construction features the three-quarter plate and the screwed gold chatons. Added to this are the different grindings and perlages that were originally meant to bind dust; today this is obsolete from a technical point of view. This combination of natural nickel silver, gold chatons, and the blued screws creates the incomparable aesthetic appearance of a Lange movement. Within traditional craftsmanship new ideas are implemented, such as the large date or the zero reset mechanism, where the seconds hand jumps to twelve and remains there until the crown is pushed again. This allows for precise time setting.

Walter Lange explains the almost mythical radiance of Lange watches: "When you hold a timepiece by A. Lange & Sons in your hands you recognize immediately that you are in the presence of something special. But to really grasp what constitutes its uniqueness you have to experience the creation of a Lange watch in its hometown: at Glashütte in Saxony. Only after you have visited the Lange factory and looked over the shoulders of master watchmakers doing their concentrated and highly complicated work do you understand how much craftsmanship, precision, and, above all, passion are contained in the timekeepers of A. Lange & Sons."

Finissage of a three-quarter plate.

Engraving the balance cock of an A. Lange & Söhne watch.

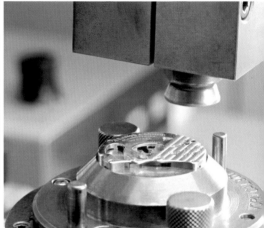

The three-quarter plate receives the Glashütte wavy grind.

During the finissage, each part of a Lange movement receives an elaborate surface finish.

The fact that these gems are offered only with precious metal cases is not surprising if you realize they would be hardly any cheaper with a stainless steel case. The labor-intensive processes, the hand-engraved balance cock, and the luxury to build a distinct movement for each model outweigh the type of case material.

Each watch, whether simple or complicated, from A. Lange & Sons is built with the highest quality standards and offers the same degree of mechanical perfection. This is also the case for a basic three-hand watch. Over sixty highly qualified employees—called finisseurs—at Lange do nothing else but the finishing of parts manufactured in-house. They master all of the techniques for the ennoblement and finishing of metal surfaces, some of which had already been forgotten. They had to be painstakingly acquired after the return of the brand in the 1990s to pass them on to new staff members. It takes at least two years for a trained watchmaker to master all of the grinding and polishing techniques. For example, take the flat polish on the escapement wheel and the escapement wheel cap jewel on a watch like the Lange 1815. Its mirror-smooth surfaces are the result of the finisseur rubbing the part on special diamond-dusted foils. To achieve an absolutely flawless flat polish, the part is placed on a support and polished in a figure-eight pattern with three increasingly fine granulations up to the finest, which is only 0.5 micrometers. This looks easy at first sight, but even the most talented finisseur requires at least six months to be somewhat confident with flat polishing. Furthermore, every step requires extreme cleanliness. One single speck of dust is all it takes to ruin several hours of work. Or the chamfer polish: here, the outer edges of the nickel silver three-quarter plate is beveled at a forty-five degree angle and is then polished with grinding paste and a rotating wooden disc. Dozens of different materials were tested at Lange until basswood (lime tree) was found to be the ideal substrate for the grinding paste when applied to nickel silver. Another challenge for the calm hand of the finisseur: the width of the chamfer must be a constant 0.2 mm across its entire length. Even the edges of the most minute orifices, such as those for letting down the mainspring, get an elaborate finish.

Many additional finishing techniques, such as circle, belt, line finish and sunburst ribbing, or the perlage, add up to a "Gesamtkunstwerk" (all-encompassing work of art) at the plant. This results in every Lange watch being an aesthetic composition of different materials and structures. Polished surfaces and edges result in beautiful reflections that can be observed via the sapphire crystal case back and increase the heartbeat of any watch connoisseur.

If you put your watch in front of these artists they will tell you after a quick look at the balance cock who in particular made your watch. As a special treat, the visitor receives an enlarged image of the balance cock with the signature of the engraver. Each watch is an entirely individual model, where the parts can not be simply swapped with a sister model. The fact that you are in the presence of precision mechanics is proven when you look at the individual parts, where the 30- to 40-mm diameter plate of a Lange 1 is its heaviest component and a ring washer of only 0.4 mm diameter and a weight of 8 micrograms (0.000008 grams) is the lightest.

The almost microscopic scale at which this is done shows the smallest drilled

Visual control at the projector. A highly magnified plate is compared with a transparent design drawing to scale.

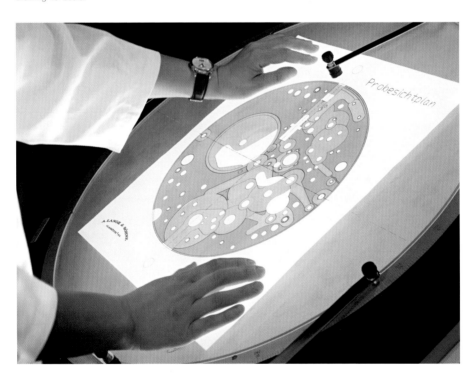

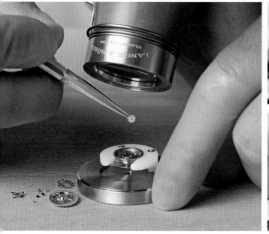

The tiny satellite impulse has to be assembled inside the snail for the tourbograph "Pour le Mérite."

A watchmaker assembles the individual parts of a chronograph.

hole located in the regulator (part of the whiplash precision index adjuster), whose diameter is a mere 0.12 mm. Lange movements of complicated watches have an incredible number of parts. The movement of a Datograph Perpetual, for example, consists of 556 parts. A close second is the Langematik Perpetual with 478, as well as the Lange Double Split and the Tourbograph "Pour le Mérite" with 465 parts each. If you were to dismantle the chain into its individual components the Tourbograph would consist of 1,097 pieces.

Even though Lange watches are not certified chronometers—this is intentionally disregarded, as the certificates are awarded exclusively by the Swiss chronometer testing facility—the test results are excellent. The tolerance for chronometer precision

is between -4 to +6 seconds (daily average). Based on experiential results, Lange prefers a setting with a maximum of -3 to +7 seconds per day. The reglage determines the precision. The task of a regleur consists of adjusting the precision via different methods so it lies within the specified tolerances. The reglage is done at Lange following three traditional steps: first, the movement of the spiral between the regulator pins—the so-called spring contact play—is adjusted. For this process the rate is measured in six positions in a fully wound state right after setting the spiral and an average rate across all positions is determined. Then the mainspring barrel is adjusted as if it had run for one day and it is measured a second time. Once again, the regleur adjusts the spring contact

Engraving still life with a drawing, various burins, and other tools.

play so that the rate in its let down state does not deviate more than three seconds average from the rate when fully wound. Then the regleur adjusts the weight of the balance to the length of the spiral spring. He places minute paired and barely visible ring washers—so-called regulating discs—under the timing screws of the balance wheel. Lastly, the balance is balanced in at least five positions. The regleur grinds away minute amounts of material from the individual timing screws until the total difference of the positions within the checked rates is under four seconds per day. The first reglage of a watch takes about two to three hours, but during the final adjustment (after mounting the movement for the second time) only a minor balancing of the balance is necessary.

Production started in 1994 with the Lange 1, and until 2011 it grew into a sizeable family of models and calibers.

Different watch models are checked for their accuracy on a watch winder.

Model: Lange 1, caliber L901.0; model: Grosse Lange 1, caliber L901.2; model: Lange 1 Mondphase (moon phase), caliber L901.5; model: Lange 1 Zeitzone (time zone), caliber L031.1; model: Saxonia, caliber L941.1; model: Saxonia Automatik, caliber L921.4; model: Grosse Saxonia Automatik, caliber L921.2; model: Richard Lange, caliber L041.2; model: Lange 31, caliber L034.1; model: Langematik Perpetual, caliber L951.1; model: Datograph Perpetual, caliber L952.1; model: Lange Double Split, caliber L001.1; model: Cabaret, caliber L931.3; model: Cabaret Mondphase, caliber L931.5; model: Cabatert Tourbillon, caliber L042.1; and model: Arkade, caliber L911.4. Other calibers can be found in the limited editions which are mostly sold out today. Model: Tourbillon "Pour le Mérite," caliber L902.0; model: Lange 1A, caliber L901.1; model: 1815 Mondphase, caliber L943.1; model: Lange 1 Tourbillon, caliber L961.1;

model: Anniversary Langematik, caliber L921.7; model: Grosse Lange 1 "Luna Mundi," caliber L901.7 + 8; model: Tourbograph "Pour le Mérite," caliber L903.0; model: 1815 Kalenderwoche (calendar week), caliber L045.1; model: Lange 31, caliber L034.1; model: Zeitwerk (timework), caliber L043.1; model: Zeitwerk "Striking Time," caliber L043.2; model: Saxonia Dual Time, caliber L086.2; and model: Richard Lange Tourbillon "Pour le Mérite," caliber L072.1.

The company strives to make as many parts as possible at its own plant. All of the parts are elaborately finished and, following the old tradition of the watchmaking craft, these are not only the parts that can later be admired through the glass back, but also those hidden inside the movement. Some fourteen different tools manufactured at the company's toolmaking facility are utilized to apply various perlages on bridges and plates. While walking around the workshops, one can observe apparently motionless watchmakers sitting at their workplace; only the index finger of the right hand makes a small circular movement. Here a specialist creates the fascinating black polish of a tourbillon bridge that will keep him busy for at least two days.

However, not only old techniques are cultivated at A. Lange & Sons. Rather, the intention is to continue developing the mechanical watch with a view towards the future. A new building was added in 2003 that houses the center for technology and development. Here the focus is on the development of proprietary balance springs, the heart of every watch.

When A. Lange & Sons was created in 1994 with the help of the IWC (International Watch Company, founded in 1868) and Jaeger-LeCoultre (founded in 1833), it still belonged to the Mannesmann Group. After its sale to Vodafone the watchmaking division was split off. In 2000, the Richemont Group, which specialized in luxury brands, bought the three brands as a package. This completed the Richemont watch section. The following brands belong to the company (the founding date in parentheses): Alfred Dunhill (1893), Montblanc (1906), Roger Dubuis (1995), Van Cleef & Arpels (1906), Piaget (1874), Cartier (1847), Officine Panerai (1860), Vacheron Constantin (1755), and Baume & Mercier (1830).

# Models and Model Series of A. Lange & Söhne - The Three-Hand Watches

## Models and Complications

THE THREE-HAND WATCHES

Lange began his fulminant restart with complication watches with outsize date and tourbillon; today, the making of traditional and sometimes unusual three-hand watches for the purist watch enthusiast is part of the program. Whether with center second hand or small seconds is left to personal taste. The first three-hand watch of the Lange production program is the model 1815, a tribute to Ferdinand Adolf Lange, who was born on February 18, 1815.

From 2009 on, the 1815 presents itself in a larger case—following the trend—as well as with a new manual winding movement. The new 1815 is also a truly classic three-hand watch with manual winding movement and is the fifth Lange model of the modern era, first presented in 1995 and with a significantly larger edition. The new 1815 combines the best virtues of the Lange art of watchmaking. With a larger 40 mm case and a new 30.6 mm diameter movement that convincingly fills the case, the new interpretation corresponds to the concept of a classic three-hand watch with a manual winding movement according to Lange's precept "Tradition, state-of-the-art." The product designers managed to conserve the well-balanced proportions of the timeless model.

With "chemin de fer" minute markers, arabic numerals, and small seconds at the six o'clock position, the new 1815 features the design characteristics of classic Lange pocket watches and carries it forward in a contemporary manner into the wristwatch format. The newly constructed Kaliber L051.1, with all of its 188 elaborately hand-decorated parts, represents the quintessence of Lange watchmaking art, such as the three-quarter plate from natural nickel silver, the hand-engraved balance cock, the whiplash precision index adjuster, and the screwed gold chatons and thermically blued screws. Inside the watch movement, a large glucydur screw balance oscillates 21,600 half-oscillations per hour. When fully wound, it offers a power reserve of fifty-five hours. The case and pin buckle of the new 1815 consist of 18-carat yellow gold, white gold, and red gold with an argenté-colored dial of solid silver. Optimal readability is provided by black numerals and typical Lange-style lanceolet-shaped hands made from blued steel. Furthermore, the watch is available in a limited edition of 500 units in a platinum case with a rhodié-colored dial and hands of rhodium-plated gold.

We owe another three-hand watch to the fact that A. Lange & Sons redefines the Saxonia, which once began with a large date. Lange grew it into a watch

1815 in red gold, white gold, yellow gold, and platinum.

1815, reference: 233.032
**Movement:** Lange manufacture caliber L051.1, manual winding. 55 hours of power reserve.
**Functions:** hour and minutes display, small seconds with seconds stop.

**Case diameter:** 40.0 mm, red gold.
**Dial:** solid silver, argenté.
**Hands:** blued steel.
**Glass and glass base:** sapphire glass.
**Strap:** hand-sewn croco band with red gold clasp.

family with three models and provides a classic, elegant, and expressive face. With cultured elegance and strong inner values, the members of the new watch family—Saxonia and Grosse Saxonia Automatik—become part of the Saxon watchmaking artistry tradition. The Saxonia was intended in reverence to Ferdinand Adolph Lange and as an expression of the close-ness with his home of Saxony when it was introduced in 1994 in the first Lange collection of the modern era at the Dresden Residenzschloss to a gaping audience. The place was carefully chosen, because the history of A. Lange & Sons had started out right here: at the court of the Saxon electors and kings. Here Ferdinand Adolph Lange began his watchmaking career as a master apprentice of the court watchmaker Gutkaes, and this was the place where the Saxon jewelry, sculpture, and watchmaking craft under August the Strong—one of Baroque's most colorful sovereigns—reached new heights. In its wake, Dresden became the Mecca of Europe's best craftsmen and the "green vault"—the court's treasure chamber—became the epitome of Saxon splendor. A current mirror image of this epoch are the three new timepieces by A. Lange & Sons whose family name Saxonia proudly refers to this tradition. Every detail of their elaborately finished movements transports the traditional values of Saxon precision watchmaking into the present.

The appearance of the Saxonia is carried by sovereign understatement. Its design is focused on the basics: the prominent lines of

Movement of the 1815, Lange manufacture caliber L051.1, manual winding, power reserve of 55 hours. Finely adjusted in five positions. Seconds stop mechanism. Plates and bridges from natural nickel silver, hand-engraved balance cock. Diameter: 30.6 mm. Height: 4.6 mm.

1815, reference: 233.026
**Movement:** Lange manufacture caliber L051.1, manual winding. Power reserve of 55 hours.
**Functions:** hour and minutes display, small seconds with seconds stop.
**Case diameter:** 40.0 mm, white gold.
**Dial:** solid silver, argenté.
**Hands:** blued steel.
**Glass and glass base:** sapphire glass.
**Strap:** hand-sewn croco band with clasp in white gold.

1815, reference: 233.025
**Movement:** Lange manufacture caliber L051.1, manual winding. Power reserve of 55 hours.
**Functions:** hour and minutes display, small seconds with seconds stop.
**Case diameter:** 40.0 mm, platinum.
**Dial:** solid silver, rhodié.
**Hands:** rhodium-plated gold
**Glass and glass base:** sapphire glass.
**Strap:** hand-sewn croco band with platinum clasp.
**Limitation:** 500 units in platinum.

1815, reference: 233.021
**Movement:** Lange manufacture caliber L051.1, manual winding. Power reserve of 55 hours.
**Functions:** hour and minutes display, small seconds with seconds stop.
**Case diameter:** 40.0 mm, yellow gold.
**Dial:** solid silver, champagne.
**Hands:** blued steel
**Glass and glass base:** sapphire glass.
**Strap:** hand-sewn croco band with yellow gold clasp.

Saxonia, reference: 215.026
**Movement:** Lange manufacture caliber L941.1, manual winding. Power reserve of 45 hours.
**Functions:** hour and minutes display, small seconds with seconds stop.
**Case diameter:** 37.0 mm, white gold.
**Dial:** solid silver, argenté.
**Hands:** rhodium-plated gold.
**Glass and glass base:** sapphire glass.
**Strap:** hand-sewn croco band with white gold clasp.

the case provide a fitting frame for the clean and perfectly readable dial. The exclusive movement with the caliber designation L941.1 can be viewed through the sapphire glass back. Its firm base frame consists of a natural nickel silver plate—an alloy mostly used at Lange these days consisting of copper, zinc, and nickel that over time develops a gold-yellow patina. The color contrast consists of the cornflower blue tempered screws and the synthetic ruby bearing jewels. Four of them are set in screwed gold chatons.

At Lange, much time and passion goes into the finissage of parts. Even surfaces that will not be visible later on are provided with elaborate polishings and ribbings. The hand-engraved balance cock ultimately

converts each watch into a unicum. The case, with a diameter of 37.0 mm, is made from 18-carat yellow, red, or white gold. The individually placed appliqués and the lanceolet-shaped hands are also made of gold. The solid silver dial is available in four colors. The large Saxonia Automatik is available with a white or red gold case and an imposing 40.6 mm diameter.

The three-hand Richard Lange is a tribute to the watch pioneer and technical director of many years at A. Lange & Sons of the same name. This watch takes up the tradition of the scientific observation watch, whose main purpose has always been its precision. For this reason the interior of a Richard Lange contains a truly masterful movement. Its characteristics

Saxonia group picture: Lange manufacture caliber L941.1 and L921.4 Sax-0-Mat. Finely adjusted in five positions. Seconds stop mechanism. Plates and bridges from natural nickel silver, hand-engraved balance cock. In white gold, yellow gold, and red gold.

Movement of the Saxonia, Lange manufacture caliber L941.1, manual winding, power reserve of 45 hours. Finely adjusted in five positions. Seconds stop mechanism. Plates and bridges from natural nickel silver, hand-engraved balance cock. Diameter: 25.6 mm. Height: 3.2 mm.

Saxonia Automatik, reference: 315.026
**Movement:** Lange manufacture caliber L.921.4 Sax-0-Mat, automatic winding, rotor is wound from both sides. Power reserve of 46 hours.
**Functions:** hour and minutes display, small seconds. Hands adjustment mechanism with patented zero reset, Lange large date display.
**Case diameter:** 37.0 mm, argenté.
**Hands:** rhodium-plated gold and blued steel.
**Glass and glass base:** sapphire glass.
**Strap:** hand-sewn croco band with white gold clasp.

Saxonia, reference: 215.021
**Movement:** Lange manufacture caliber L941.1, manual winding. Power reserve of 45 hours.
**Functions:** hour and minutes display, small seconds with seconds stop.
**Case diameter:** 37.0 mm, yellow gold.
**Dial:** solid silver, champagne.
**Hands:** yellow gold.
**Glass and glass base:** sapphire glass.
**Strap:** hand-sewn croco band with yellow gold clasp.

Richard Lange, reference: 232.032
**Movement:** Lange manufacture caliber L041.2, manual winding. Power reserve of 38 hours.
**Functions:** hour and minutes display, central seconds with seconds stop.
**Case diameter:** 40.5 mm, red gold.
**Dial:** solid silver, argenté.
**Hands:** red gold and blued steel.
**Glass and glass base:** sapphire glass.
**Strap:** hand-sewn croco band with red gold clasp.

include an elaborate oscillation system without a regulator with a large eccentric balance and a balance spiral developed and manufactured in-house. It runs with 21,600 half-oscillations and is affixed with a patented spiral clamp that allows for easier future regulation adjustments.

The balance spiral is perhaps Richard Lange's main accomplishment, for which he applied a patent in 1930 under the label "metal alloy for watch springs." A scientific study published at the end of the 1920s about beryllium-nickel alloys, where the quenching and tempering properties of a small amount of beryllium were described, prompted him to recognize the usability of these scientific results for the watchmaking industry. He realized that the addition of beryllium to nickel steel alloys reduced sensitivity of the spiral to changes in temperature and magnetic fields while its elasticity and hardness when compared to the common Elinvar spirals could be increased.

Although Richard Lange, who died two years after the patent was granted, could not undertake the technical realization of his invention, he provided the decisive foundation for the composition of the material that is still used today.

Today, Lange manufactures balance springs with the most modern production methods for its own watch movements—one of the world's few manufacturing plants

Richard Lange, reference: 232.025
**Movement:** Lange manufacture caliber L041.2, manual winding. Power reserve of 38 hours.
**Functions:** hour and minutes display, central seconds with seconds stop.
**Case diameter:** 40.5 mm, platinum
**Dial:** solid silver, rhodié.
**Hands:** rhodium-plated gold and blued steel.
**Glass and glass base:** sapphire glass.
**Strap:** hand-sewn croco band with platinum clasp.

to do so. All of this benefits Richard Lange. For several years, the Lange laboratory searched for and investigated to find the best possible combination of balance wheel and balance spiral and to perfectly match these parts that are decisive for the rate of a watch. Added to this is the application of a position where only the most constant part of the torque curve of the tension spring is active. With the help of a separate measurement with a special vibration measuring device it was possible to isolate the influences of the escapement and the geartrain on the rate.

The selected construction and the precise adjustment of the oscillating system ensure that the rate deviation of the watch is within extremely narrow tolerances. Everything that contributed to the highest possible rate precision via mechanical means was applied.

This reinterpretation of the scientific observation watch—the Richard Lange—follows the tradition of the scientific pocket observation watches. This began long before the military discovered the observation watch because of its precision and turned it into a functional item, and it can point to famous paragons from its own company. The high-quality handmade pocket watches of A. Lange & Sons were not only famous and much sought after from the second half of the nineteenth century onwards because of their many useful innovations and complications, but particularly because of their extraordinarily precise rate. In those times astronomy and physics, as well as the new means of transportation, such as railway and airplanes, depended on the precise measurement of time.

Until the time signals were sent into the ether via radio after 1913, the precise time had to be sent from observatories with the help of pocket observation watches into the field of operation; for example, to a ship and its marine chronometer. During the first German Antarctic expedition led by Erich von Drygalski from 1901 to 1903, six precision pocket watches made by A. Lange & Sons were purchased for measuring time on board the research vessel *Gauss*. Lange development of precision watches reached its zenith with the "Grosse Beobachtungsuhr" ("Large Observation Watch") with a 57 mm movement diameter; only fifteen units were made between 1917 and 1937. It went to prestigious addresses, such as the Gesellschaft für Zeitmesskunde (Society for the Measurement of Time) in Berlin, the Zeppelin shipyard in Friedrichshafen, or the Physikalische Institut der Bergakademie (Physical Institute of the Bergakademie) Clausthal-Zellerfeld.

Due to the larger diameter of the pocket observation watches a better readability was achieved—a requirement that observation watches always had to

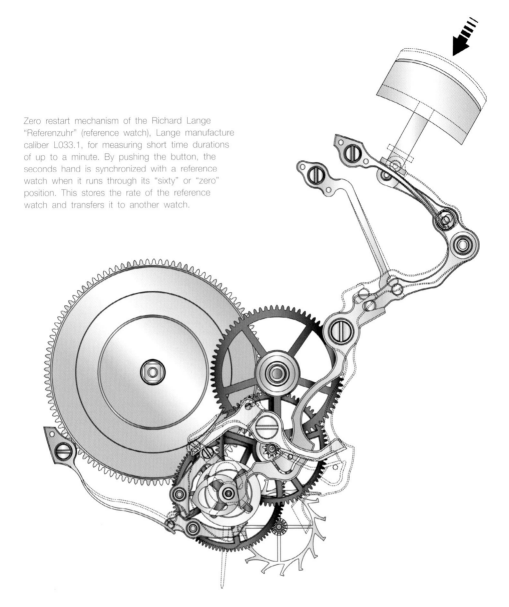

Zero restart mechanism of the Richard Lange "Referenzuhr" (reference watch), Lange manufacture caliber L033.1, for measuring short time durations of up to a minute. By pushing the button, the seconds hand is synchronized with a reference watch when it runs through its "sixty" or "zero" position. This stores the rate of the reference watch and transfers it to another watch.

fulfill, apart from very narrow rate tolerances. This tradition is picked up masterfully with the Richard Lange. Its appearance is convincing, with its sixfold screwed case of 18-carat gold or platinum and a 40.5 mm diameter matched to the wrist's proportions. The solid silver dial features slim Roman numerals as used earlier for this type of watch. The blued central seconds hand precisely transfers the split seconds onto the scale. Precision minute markers with 1/6 second steps indicate Lange designers took it rather seriously to build a timekeeper for the highest standards. The seconds counter wheel is driven by a separate geartrain. The movement features a seconds stop—a "must" for every observation watch. When pulling the crown, the balance is locked and the seconds hand stops immediately. This allows for setting the watch to the timing signal.

Other features of the watch movement include a fine adjustment of the drop-off timing with a whiplash spring. An additional geartrain with a bridge for the central second hand increases the height of the exclusive movement a total of 6.0 mm. The movement is precisely adjusted by master watchmakers at Lange in five positions. The movement of the Richard Lange is elaborately decorated and visible through the sapphire glass back. The Kaliber L041.2 with the blued steel screws, screwed gold chatons, hand-engraved balance cock, plates of natural nickel silver, and the elaborate finissage of all of the 199 individual parts is a convincing reinterpretation of the scientific observation watch and provides this rightfully famous watch type with a glamorous renaissance.

With the Richard Lange "Referenzuhr" (reference watch)—featuring a zero restart function and a new seconds reset func-tion—the series named after Richard Lange is complemented by an extraordinary three-hand watch. When a push-piece above the crown is activated its seconds

Richard Lange "Referenzuhr" (reference watch), reference: 250.032
**Movement:** Lange manufacture caliber L033.1, manual winding. Power reserve of 38 hours.
**Functions:** hour and minutes display, small seconds with zero restart function, power reserve indicator.
**Case diameter:** 40.5 mm, red gold.
**Dial:** red gold and blued steel.
**Glass and glass base:** sapphire glass.
**Strap:** hand-sewn croco band with red gold clasp.
**Limitation:** 75 in red gold.

Richard Lange "Referenzuhr," reference: 250.025
**Movement:** Lange manufacture caliber L033.1,
manual winding. Power reserve of 38 hours.
**Functions:** hour and minutes display, small seconds
with zero restart function, power reserve indicator.
**Case diameter:** 40.5 mm, platinum.
**Dial:** solid silver, rhodié.
**Hands:** rhodium-plated gold and blued steel.
**Glass and glass base:** sapphire glass.
**Strap:** hand-sewn croco band with platinum clasp.
**Limitation:** 50 in platinum.

hand jumps to zero and stays in this position for as long as the button is held down. Meanwhile, a vertical disc clutch makes sure timekeeping is not interrupted and that the movement continues. When the button is released the seconds hand immediately continues. This zero restart function is very valuable for short time measurements of up to one minute or to synchronize separate watches: by pressing the push-piece the seconds hand is synchronized with that of a reference watch when it passes the "sixty" or "zero" position. This stores the current rate of the reference watch, which can then be transferred to another watch. The Richard Lange "Referenzuhr" is a tribute to a citadel of the art of timekeeping that played an important role in the nineteenth century: the time service of the Mathematical-Physical Salon. As a "Keeper of Time," this scientific institution was in charge of determining the precise local time and providing it to the population of Dresden. As such, it was a forerunner of contemporary atomic watches and time signal transmitters.

The difficulty in determining the correct time is hard to grasp in the modern era, where we live with an abundance

of time: in those days time had to be calculated on the basis of astronomical calculations. The result was then transferred to a precision pendulum watch. With this reference time and with the help of particularly precise precision pocket watches, the time was then set on the clocks in public squares, in administrative buildings, and other locations that relied on the exact time. The clients of the time service included astronomers and watchmakers, as well as the then developing railway system.

Movement of the Richard Lange "Referenzuhr," Lange manufacture caliber L033.1, manual winding, power reserve of 38 hours. Finely adjusted in five positions. Zero restart mechanism, patented seconds stop mechanism. Plates and bridges from natural nickel silver; hand-engraved balance cock. Diameter: 30.6 mm. Height: 6.8 mm.

The layout of the dial of the Richard Lange reference watch, with its eccentric small seconds, references a historical model from 1811: a pocket chronometer that was proven to be utilized for the synchronization of the time service. It originates from Johann Heinrich Seyffert, who furthered precision watchmaking in Dresden like no other watchmaker. His most famous customer was the natural scientist Alexander von Humboldt, who purchased a chronometer for his extensive South America expedition.

With six half oscillations per second, a large eccentric balance, and the balance spring developed and manufactured at Lange, the Richard Lange "Referenzuhr" provides the precision expected from a timekeeper serving scientific purposes. A view through the sapphire glass base is a real treat for enthusiasts of technical finesse: the zero restart lever mechanism is visible on the three-quarter plate, just like the geartrain of the winding mechanism. This watch is already an extraordinary collector's item.

Winding mechanism of the Richard Lange "Referenzuhr" (reference watch), caliber L033.1, visibly mounted on the three-quarter plate.

# From the Small to the Large Complication

## The Complications at A. Lange & Söhne

### LARGE DATE (Grossdatum)
- Lange 1
- Cabaret
- Arkade
- Saxonia Jahreskalender
- Lange 1 Daymatic

### POWER RESERVE INDICATOR (Gangreserveanzeige)
- Lange 1
- 1815 Auf und Ab (up and down)

### TOURBILLON
- Lange 1-Tourbillon
(2000-2003)
- "Pour le Mérite"
(1994-1998)
- Cabaret Tourbillon
- Lange 1-Tourbillon
Homage to F.A. Lange

### IMPULSE VIA FUSEE AND CHAIN
- Tourbograph "Pour le Mérite"
- Tourbillon "Pour le Mérite"
(1994-1998)
- Richard Lange "Pour le Mérite"
- Richard Lange Tourbillon "Pour le Mérite"

### CHRONOGRAPHS
- Datograph
- 1815 Chronograph
- Chronograph Double Split

### CALENDAR AND PERPETUAL CALENDAR
- Langematik Perpetual
- Datograph Perpetual
- Saxonia Jahreskalender (yearly calendar)

### WORLD TIME WATCH (Weltzeituhr)
- Lange 1 Zeitzone (time zone)

# LARGE DATE:

## Lange 1, Cabaret, Arkade, Saxonia Jahreskalender (yearly calendar), Lange 1 Daymatic

One complication which caught the eye at the presentation of the new Lange watches was the large date. For the expert, complications are all the functions of a watch that go beyond the scope of a conventional three-hand watch. There is a distinction between large and small complication. The latter might be a power reserve or a date display. The large com-

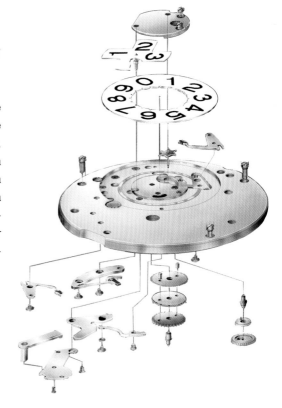

Illustration of the elaborate mechanism of the Lange large date, consisting of program discs and latching elements. The large date consists of sixty-eight tiny precision parts.

Grosse Lange 1 (Big Lange 1), Lange manufacture caliber L901.2, manual winding, power reserve of 72 hours. Finely adjusted in five positions; double barrel, a patented two-disc mechanism to show the large display, seconds stop mechanism. Plates and bridges from natural nickel silver. Hand-engraved balance cock.
In yellow gold, red gold, and platinum.

Rear view of the Lange 1 movement.

Lange 1, reference: 101.325
**Movement:** Lange manufacture caliber L901.0,
manual winding. Power reserve of 72 hours.
**Functions:** asymmetric hour and minutes indicator,
small seconds with seconds stop, Lange large date
display. Power reserve indicator auf/ab (up/down).
**Case diameter:** 38.5 mm, platinum.
**Dial:** solid silver, rhodié.
**Hands:** rhodium-plated gold.
**Glass and glass base:** sapphire glass.
**Strap:** high-quality metal strap in platinum.

Lange 1 reference: 101.039
**Movement:** Lange manufacture caliber L901.0,
manual winding. Power reserve of 72 hours.
**Functions:** asymmetric hour and minutes display,
small seconds with seconds stop, Lange large date
display. Power reserve indicator auf/ab (up/down).
**Case diameter:** 38.5 mm, white gold.
**Dial:** solid silver, argenté.
**Hands:** rhodium-plated gold.
**Glass and glass base:** sapphire glass.
**Strap:** hand-sewn croco band with white gold clasp.

plications, such as perpetual calendar, tourbillon, or striking mechanism, however, require supreme watchmaking expertise. This results in an increasing miniaturization of the displays, as available space on the dial of a wristwatch is rather limited. With decreasing eyesight they are often only readable for older people when using glasses or magnifying glasses. In this respect, the large date is not only a rediscovery and an improved realization of a forgotten idea. After all, the date was now five times larger when compared to wristwatches. The application of the Lange patent is based on a new two-disc mechanism: one of them is a ring-shaped disc printed with numerals 0 to 9, and on top of it lies the cross-shaped month disc with numerals 1 to 3 and an empty panel. When the discs are moved

Lange 1 reference: 101.032
**Movement:** Lange manufacture caliber L901.0, manual winding. Power reserve of 72 hours.
**Functions:** asymmetric hour and minutes display, small seconds with seconds stop, Lange large date display. Power reserve indicator auf/ab (up/down).
**Case diameter:** 38.5 mm, red gold.
**Dial:** solid silver, argenté.
**Hands:** red gold.
**Glass and glass base:** sapphire glass.
**Strap:** hand-sewn croco band with red gold clasp.

Lange 1, reference: 101.025
**Movement:** Lange manufacture caliber L901.0, manual winding. Power reserve of 72 hours.
**Functions:** asymmetric hour and minutes display, small seconds with seconds stop, Lange large date display. Power reserve indicator auf/ab (up/down).
**Glass and glass base:** sapphire glass.
**Strap:** hand-sewn croco band with platinum clasp.

stepwise they automatically show 1 to 31. After that, the 1 remains fixed and the tens disc moves forward to the empty panel or slot. The model for this type of display is the famous five-minute watch of the Semper opera that Johann-Christian Gutkaes—father-in-law of company found-

er Ferdinand Adolph Lange—built in his capacity as royal court watchmaker.

The Arkade and Cabaret rectangular models embody one of the most important principles of the A. Lange & Sons watch philosophy. It posits that only a movement designed and made at Lange is allowed

Lange 1, reference: 101.021
**Movement:** Lange manufacture caliber
L901.0, manual winding. Power reserve of
72 hours.
**Functions:** asymmetric hour and minutes
display, small seconds with seconds stop,
Lange large date display. Power reserve
indicator auf/ab (up/down).
**Case diameter:** 38.5 mm, yellow gold.
**Dial:** solid silver, champagne.
**Hands:** yellow gold
**Glass and glass base:** sapphire glass.
**Strap:** hand-sewn croco band with yellow
gold clasp.

Grosse (big) Lange 1, reference: 115.032
**Movement:** Lange manufacture caliber L901.2,
manual winding. Power reserve of 72 hours.
**Functions:** asymmetric hour and minutes display,
small seconds with seconds stop, power reserve
indicator.
**Case diameter:** 41.9 mm, red gold.
**Dial:** solid silver, argenté.
**Hands:** red gold.
**Glass and glass base:** sapphire glass.
**Strap:** hand-sewn croco band with red gold clasp.

Form movement of the Cabaret; for comparison, a date ring from conventional movements.

Big Arkade, reference: 106.021
**Movement:** Lange manufacture caliber L911.4, manual winding. Power reserve of 42 hours.
**Functions:** hour and minutes display, small seconds with seconds stop, Lange large date display.
**Case diameter:** 38.0 mm, yellow gold.
**Dial:** solid silver, champagne.
**Hands:** yellow gold.
**Glass and glass base:** sapphire glass.
**Strap:** hand-sewn croco band with yellow gold clasp.

Big Arkade Jewelry, reference: 801.021
**Movement:** Lange manufacture caliber L911.4, manual winding. Power reserve of 42 hours.
**Functions:** hour and minutes display, small seconds with seconds stop, Lange large date display.
**Case:** 38.0 mm, yellow gold. Bezel set with 40 brilliants.
**Dial:** solid silver, champagne.
**Hands:** yellow gold
**Glass and glass base:** sapphire glass.
**Strap:** hand-sewn croco band with yellow gold clasp.

to tick inside a timekeeper of the Saxon company. Hence in the case of the cabaret, the existing Kaliber L911.4 movement, at 25.6 x 17.6 mm and a height of 4.95 mm, was not utilized, but rather the new L931.3 movement. Both manual winding mechanisms tick with 21,600 oscillations, have a power reserve of forty-two hours, and feature the identical shape of their cases, forming a homogenous unit. This can be verified by looking through the sapphire glass base.

No other Lange watch features the large date in such a surprising and dominant way. The observer asks how this display was done technically, as a date circle with numerals this size would have a diameter much larger than the size of the watch. Both models allow for setting the date via a corrective button at the two. While the production of the Arkade was stopped, the Cabaret continues to be built almost without change; it is even complemented by a model with moon phase and a tourbillon. The strive for perfection is served by the fact that the cabaret—as a rectangular watch—features its own custom-made movement that fills the slim case—even in the most hidden corners—with well thought out mechanics and the finest Lange watchmaking artistry. This allowed for a particularly elegant case and a balanced dial independent of the dimensions of its round watch movement, which would

be either too wide or not high enough to accommodate all of the features in a harmonious way.

While the Saxonia models have managed without a large date but feature a yearly calendar, the first Saxonia Automatik featured—apart from all the quality features which characterize the noble Saxonia family—a large date display.

Furthermore, an extraordinary watch movement works inside: the famous Lange calibre Sax-0-Mat. While the first and last syllable of the name indicate the geographic origin of Saxony and the automatic winding mechanism, the "zero" in the middle stands for the technically sophisticated zero reset mechanism. It causes the seconds hand to immediately reset to zero when pulling the crown, which greatly simplifies synchronization with a timing signal. The claim to technical uniqueness is supported by the Sax-0-Mat-Kaliber's winding mechanism: the delicately embossed rotor made from gold and platinum winds up the watch via a geartrain from both sides. Four ball bearings make sure that its torque is transferred with maximum efficiency onto the winding spring. The gear ratio is calculated so that even in the case of a calm wearer there is always a sufficient power reserve being built up. The winding rotor and escapement can be viewed through the glass base while doing their fascinating work.

The rectangular Cabaret features the large date particularly nicely. Originally this red gold variation with a red sewn leather strap was supposed to be called "black, red, gold."

The face of the Saxonia Automatik is characterized by the centrally located Lange large date indicator below the twelve.

Since its premiere, the Lange 1 has featured the unmistakable look of A. Lange & Sons. The off-center dial design and its patented large date display provide an iconic design with high recognition value. It is also one of the most awarded watches of all time and the most successful timepiece of this tradition-rich company. Its triumph stimulated the development of an entire product family of six models which, with all their individuality, have one thing in common: a manual winding mechanism with a twin mainspring barrel and a power reserve of three days

Cabaret Tourbillon, reference: 703.032
**Movement:** Lange manufacture caliber L042.1, manual winding. Power reserve of five days.
**Functions:** minutes tourbillon with patented seconds stop. Hour and minutes display, small seconds, Lange large date display, power reserve indicator auf/ab (up/down).
**Case:** 39.2 x 29.5 mm, red gold.
**Dial:** solid silver, argenté.
**Hands:** red gold.
**Glass and glass base:** sapphire glass.
**Strap:** hand-sewn croco band with red gold clasp.

Cabaret Tourbillon, reference: 703.032
**Movement:** Lange manufacture caliber L042.1, manual winding. Power reserve of five days.
**Functions:** minutes tourbillon with patented seconds stop. Hour and minutes display, small seconds, Lange large date display, power reserve indicator auf/ab (up/down).
**Case:** 39.2 x 29.5 mm, red gold.
**Dial:** solid silver, argenté.
**Hands:** red gold.
**Glass and glass base:** sapphire glass.
**Strap:** hand-sewn croco band with red gold clasp.

Cabaret Tourbillon, reference: 703.025
**Movement:** Lange manufacture caliber L042.1, manual winding. Power reserve of five days.
**Functions:** minutes tourbillon with patented seconds stop. Hour and minutes display, small seconds, Lange large date display, power reserve indicator auf/ab (up/down).
**Case:** 39.2 x 29.5 mm, platinum
**Dial:** solid silver, rhodié.
**Hands:** rhodium-plated gold.
**Glass and glass base:** sapphire glass.
**Strap:** hand-sewn croco band with platinum clasp.

Lange 1 Daymatic with automatic winding and
Lange 1 with manual winding in yellow gold.

with a progressive power reserve indicator. So far there was no automatic movement available for the watch.

For all those who would like to have a watch with an automatic winding mechanism, the wait is now over. The Lange 1 Daymatic with automatic winding mechanism also features a retrograde week display. At first sight this watch looks familiar, but looking closer, it turns out to be innovative in every respect. With an automatic movement developed from the ground up, this watch allows for a new perspective and a new look at the Lange 1. The dial of the Lange 1 Daymatic, when compared to the manual Lange 1, is designed as a mirror image. Only a connoisseur notices the discreet difference on the automatic Lange 1. Its main dial, with hour and minutes indicator, is now located on the right side. For the majority of watch enthusiasts who wear their watch on their left wrist, this arrangement means the eye catches the most important information first: the time. On the other hand, the patented large date was removed from its customary location at the top right and placed on the left side. It is complemented by the retrograde week display below. It replaces the power reserve

indicator unnecessary for an automatic watch. Date and week display can be easily set independently of each other via two buttons.

Just as in the case of the classic Lange 1, the Lange 1 Daymatic has harmoniously arranged indicators on its solid silver dial. The center of the large date and the pointer shafts of days and seconds display lie on a vertical line. It

Lange 1 Daymatic, available in yellow gold, red gold, and platinum. Caliber L021.1, automatic winding, central rotor with platinum flywheel mass. Time display with hour and minutes, small seconds with seconds stop, patented large date, and retrograde day display.

Lange 1 Daymatic, reference: 320.032
**Movement:** Lange manufacture caliber L021.1, automatic winding. Power reserve of 50 hours.
**Functions:** asymmetric hour and minutes display, small seconds with seconds stop, Lange large date display, retrograde day display.
**Case diameter:** 39.5 mm, red gold.
**Dial:** solid silver, argenté.
**Hands:** red gold.
**Glass and glass base:** sapphire glass.
**Strap:** hand-sewn croco band with red gold clasp.

Lange 1 Daymatic, reference: 320.025
**Movement:** Lange manufacture caliber L021.1,
automatic winding.
Power reserve of 50 hours.
**Functions:** asymmetric hour and minutes display,
small seconds with seconds stop, Lange large
date display, retrograde day display.
**Case diameter:** 39.5 mm, platinum.
**Dial:** rhodium-plated gold.
**Glass and glass base:** sapphire glass.
**Strap:** hand-sewn croco band with platinum clasp.

forms the basis of an isosceles triangle whose tip precisely meets the center of the main dial.

The solid yellow gold, red gold, or platinum case of the Lange 1 Daymatic has grown one millimeter with respect to the classic Lange 1, to an impressive 39.5 mm. Its interior contains an entirely newly developed movement: the automatic caliber number L021.1. A central rotor finely embossed with the "A. Lange & Söhne" legend takes care of its effective winding, taking the entire diameter of the movement at 31.6 mm. The flywheel mass at the outer edge of the rotor made from platinum ensures that even the slightest movement of the wrist is converted into power reserve. After fully winding a power reserve of fifty hours is available. Additional quality features of the movement include a hand-engraved balance cock and a regulator-less oscillating system with a large eccentric balance, as well as the balance spiral, which is designed and manufactured in-house.

The crowning conclusion of this Lange craftsmanship consists of seven screwed gold chatons held in place by thermically blued screws. Precious features such as these are the genetic fingerprint that clearly identify the Lange 1 Daymatic as a member of the unique Lange 1 family. The yearly calendar of the Saxonia series features a calender display that only requires correction in February. It provides all of the essential

information at a single glance: hour, minutes and seconds, day of the week, date, month, and moon phase. The moon phase display is so accurate that it would have to be reset back one day every 122 years if it were to run that long without interruption.

Lange 1 Daymatic, reference: 320.021
**Movement:** Lange manufacture caliber L021.1, automatic winding.
Power reserve of 50 hours.
**Functions:** asymmetric hour and minutes display, small seconds with seconds stop, Lange large date display, retrograde day display.
**Case diameter:** 39.5 mm, yellow gold.
**Dial:** solid silver, champagne.
**Hands:** yellow gold.
**Glass and glass base:** sapphire glass.
**Strap:** hand-sewn croco band with yellow gold clasp.

# POWER RESERVE DISPLAY:
## *Lange 1, 1815 Auf und Ab (Up and Down)*

The power reserve display is a small complication found on many Lange watches, usually in combination with other complications up to the tourbillon. Watches with a power reserve display, such as the 1815 "Auf und Ab" (up and down) presented in 1997, are quite rare, but in the case of the Lange 1, the large date is also the main complication. Depending on the duration of the power reserve, the display indicates those hours or

Special version of the 1815 "Auf und Ab" (up and down) for Japan and the US "W. Lange" inside the flip lid. Limited to fifty units.

days when the watch must be wound up again. In the case of the Glashütte "Auf und Ab" movement, this complication is integrated via a small planetary gear into the watch movement and connected both to the barrel and the winding mechanism. This is also true for the Kaliber L942.1 of the 1815 "Auf und Ab," which was mostly constructed anew and features over forty-six additional parts just for the power reserve display. This is distinctive from the modular technique often used in Swiss movements. The tourbillon "Pour le Mérite" also features the rather useful power reserve display, which comes handy for manually wound watches like the Lange Zeitwerk, the Lange 1 Zeitzone, the Cabaret Tourbillon, the tourbograph "Pour le Mérite," or the Double Split chronograph.

# TOURBILLON:

*Lange 1 Tourbillon (2000—2003), "Pour le Mérite" (1994-1998), Cabaret Tourbillon, Lange 1 Tourbillon Homage to F.A. Lange*

For centuries and to the present, watchmakers have striven to improve the rate precision of watches. Although we do not know of a mechanical machine that runs more precisely than a watch movement, there are several factors that add up to a fatal source of errors for the small, wondrous movement: differences in temperature, the imbalance of individual parts, and the force of gravity all play a part, particularly in the case of vertically-worn pocket watches, where position errors are quite noticeable.

A simple yet technically challenging solution was to build the anchor, escapement wheel, and balance so that the ensemble turns around itself. This idea goes back to Abraham-Louis Breguet (1747—1823), who made this discovery around 1795 and patented it in 1801. However, only a few watchmakers are capable of realizing this elaborate technique: in Germany, Alfred Helwig and A. Lange & Sons are among them, with their tourbillon designs creating a worldwide sensation. The "flying tourbillon" developed by

Movement of the Lange 1 tourbillon "Pour le Mérite" from the "165 Years - Homage to F. A. Lange Collection 2010," Lange manufacture caliber L961.2, manual winding, power reserve of 72 hours. Finely adjusted in five positions. Lange spiral, patented two-disc mechanics for displaying the large date, minutes tourbillon with patented seconds stop mechanism. Plates and bridges from natural nickel silver, crown wheel balance with ray grind, intermediate wheel and tourbillon balance from honey-colored gold, hand-engraved. Diameter: 38.5 mm. Height: 9.8 mm.

Helwig allows for an undisturbed view of the tourbillon due to its suspension on one side.

Although wristwatch movements were part of chronometer competitions in the 1950s and 1960s and were partially successful, the tourbillon was included quite late in a commercially available wristwatch during the renaissance of mechanics in 1986 due to the Swiss manufacturer Audemars Piguet. Although it can be worked with machines, the tourbillon today is still among the most expensive mechanical complications. The high status of this complication is acknowledged at A. Lange & Sons by the fact that these are built in their highest-quality Lange watches.

After the tourbillon overture of the "Pour le Mérite" there was another watch with this complication, the following Lange 1 Tourbillon. Built from 2000 to 2003, it is the world's first and only tourbillon wristwatch featuring a large date display, a twin mainspring barrel for three days of power reserve, and a progressive power reserve display. The tourbillon frame of this watch is supported at the front by a highly polished steel cock precisely fitted into the solid silver dial that conforms to the most characteristic design element of this Lange 1. The small seconds fits perfectly into the asymmetric arrangement of the displays.

Every detail shows the highly developed sense for harmonious proportions that has contributed to this watch being a classic with a distinct appearance. The solid silver dial is laid out in three layers and—depending on the model —features rhodium-plated or red gold appliqués. The hands are made of gold. The sapphire glass and the sapphire glass base have an anti-glare treatment. The watch movement of the Lange 1 Tourbillon, Kaliber L961.1—consisting of 378 individual hand-crafted parts—combines everything that provides modern Lange watches with their comet-like rise and constitute the special character of these watches: plates and bridges from cross-rolled natural nickel silver, screwed gold chatons, screw balance, and hand-engraved bridges. It features forty-nine rubies and two diamond bearing jewels, a shock-proofed balance, a Nivarox-1 spiral with bent terminal curve, and 21,600 half-oscillations per hour. This watch was limited to 150 platinum watches and 250 watches in red gold and is only found with antiques vendors.

A. Lange & Sons managed for the first time in the history of watchmaking to tame the "whirlwind"—the literal translation for tourbillon—with a stop seconds in the new Kaliber L042.1. But let's not get ahead of ourselves: the invention of the tourbillon escapement, patented in 1801, is based on an ingenious idea. It was designed for

pocket watches worn in the vest pocket, upright and always in the same position. Because the parts that determine the rate—balance and escapement—turn around the fixed seconds wheel inside a cage rack, the positional error caused by the influence of the earth's gravity on the never-perfectly-balanced balance could be compensated for, leading to increased rate precision. Even if the necessity for rate correction for today's wristwatches—worn in continuously changing positions—is first and foremost anymore, the tourbillon, with its filigree complexity, has not lost any of its original fascination. With consummate craftsmanship, these three tourbillon calibers from the Lange company are still the epitome of precision mechanics complication, only mastered by the best of the watchmaking elite.

Movement of the Cabaret Tourbillon, Lange manufacture caliber L042.1, manual winding, power reserve of five days. Finely adjusted in five positions. Patented two-disc mechanics for displaying the large date, minutes tourbillon with patented seconds stop mechanism. Plates and bridges from natural nickel silver, hand-engraved intermediate wheel and tourbillon balance. Diameter: 32.6 x 22.3 mm. Height: 6.35 mm.

The Lange 1 Tourbillon in platinum was only
available in a limited edition of 150 units. The
manual winding mechanism L961.1 is only 5.9 mm
high. Apart from the tourbillon, the watch features
the Lange large date and a power reserve
indicator at the three o'clock position. The watch
was manufactured 250 times in red gold.

One question remains unanswered: if the tourbillon stands for highly precise rates, why was it not possible to come up with a mechanism to stop such a watch and set it precisely. Unanswered in the 200-year history of the tourbillon, this question challenged the designers at Lange, and they ultimately found an original solution. The possibility to mechanically stop the entire tourbillon cage was discarded, because this rather simple solution would cause the balance to oscillate out of its mechanism and eventually lose its energy. It would require an outside impulse for it to restart. To maintain the potential energy at the moment of stoppage only a direct, delay-free braking of the balance rotating inside the cage itself was an option. This solution would enable the balance to immediately oscillate again after applying the "brake."

But how should one stop an oscillating balance of a tourbillon escapement in a turning cage when one of the three pillars of the cage is in the way every twenty seconds? Until now, all of the specialists dedicated to tourbillon escapements had capitulated, leaving the designers at Lange

Stop mechanism of the Cabaret Tourbillon, Lange manufacture caliber L042.1. Stop spring of the patented seconds stop mechanism for the tourbillon.

to find the answer more than two centuries after the invention of the tourbillon: the pulling of the crown activates a complex lever movement that places the stop lever, with two V-shaped bent spring levers, onto the outer balance wheel and hence immediately stops the balance. This action is complicated by the fact that the V-shaped braking spring might hit one of the three pillars of the tourbillon cage with one of its arms, so the delicate steel stopping spring is mounted in a movable manner on one of the rotation points of the braking lever via both of its arms.

This means that one of the spring arms rests on the cage pillar while the other lowers itself onto the outer face of the balance and stops it as reliably as if both spring arms had met the balance wheel.

The asymmetric curved shape of the two ends of the spring was determined during a long series of experiments. They are shaped so they exert optimal pressure at all positions of the balance to the braking spring. Furthermore, the ends of the braking spring are bent so they cannot become stuck when stopping and releasing the balance. This is not only an intelligent

Lange 1 Tourbillon "Homage to F.A. Lange,"
reference: 722.050
**Movement:** Lange manufacture caliber L961.2,
manual winding. Power reserve of 72 hours.
**Functions:** asymmetric hour and minutes display,
minutes tourbillon with patented seconds stop.
Power reserve indicator auf/ab (up/down).
**Case diameter:** 38.5 mm, honey-colored gold.
**Dial:** solid gold, argenté, guilloché.
**Hands:** honey-colored gold.
**Glass and glass base:** sapphire glass.
**Strap:** hand-sewn croco band with clasp in
honey-colored gold.
**Limitation:** 150 units.

complication prominently and aesthetically presented on the dial side of the Cabaret Tourbillon, it is also a useful innovation in the best Lange tradition, because the patented invention finally makes it possible to precisely measure the improved rate performance of the tourbillon.

The Cabaret Tourbillon offers additional special features: the twin mainspring barrel of the newly developed manual winding caliber L042.1 retains a power reserve of five days or 120 hours after being fully wound. A power reserve display at four o'clock reliably reminds the owner when it is time to provide his masterpiece with new energy. The famous Lange large date below the twelve constitutes the visual counterbalance to the tourbillon visible via a notch in the dial. The form movement, made and finished with the highest Lange quality criteria, is a veritable feast for the eye: six screwed gold chatons are distributed on the finely decorated three-quarter plate made from nickel silver. Three additional chatons are located on the hand-engraved intermediate wheel and tourbillon cock, as well as on the tourbillon bridge, which is finished with a black ribbing on the dial side. The pivots of the balance rim are held by two diamond endstones. Apart from forty-five ruby bearing jewels, they are not only an indication of the watchmaking excellence of this movement, but also sovereign references to traditional watchmaking craftsmanship that had earlier distinguished the highest quality category 1A Lange pocket watches. A rectangular platinum or red gold case measuring 29.5 by 39.2 mm provides the perfect frame for the world premiere of the first tourbillon with stop seconds. Lange's ingenious solution to the problem—the patented stop seconds mechanism—can now be found in the Lange 1 Tourbillon of the anniversary collection 165 Years. It can be observed via the transparent sapphire glass one-ring of the large date.

# IMPULSE VIA FUSEE-CHAIN TRANSMISSION:

*Tourbograph "Pour le Mérite" (1994-1994), Tourbillon "Pour le Mérite" (1994-1998), Richard Lange "Pour le Mérite", Richard Lange Tourbillon "Pour le Mérite"*

Tourbograph "Pour le Mérite," reference: 702.025 F
**Movement:** Lange manufacture caliber L903.0, manual winding. Minutes tourbillon with impulse via fusee and chain. Power reserve of 36 hours.
**Functions:** hour and minutes display, chronograph-rattrapante.
Power reserve display.
**Case diameter:** 41.2 mm, platinum.
**Dial:** blued steel and gilded.
**Glass and glass base:** sapphire glass.
**Strap:** hand-sewn croco band with platinum clasp.
**Limitation:** 51 units.

Every part of the Lange movement receives an elaborate surface finish. Here, the perlage of a wheel bridge of the Tourbograph "Pour le Mérite."

Pre-assembly: the gold chaton with inserted diamond endstone is mounted with two screws to the tourbillon bridge of the Tourbograph "Pour le Mérite."

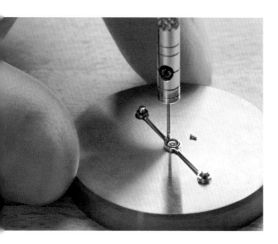

The balance of the Tourbograph "Pour le Mérite" is adjusted with a steady hand.

Lange offered a surprise with its first collection in 1994 with a tourbillon featuring winding via fusee-chain as an additional complication. With the tourbograph "Pour le Mérite," presented in 2005, Lange offered a watch that had never existed before. The watch features two classic complications that contribute to its precision. On the one hand, this is a minute tourbillon, while on the other the impulse via fusee-chain, and all in the format of a wristwatch. Truly a large complication, the watch also features a rattrapante chronograph. More than the tourbillon, which equalizes the influence of gravity, the impulse via fusee-chain balances the different torques at the beginning and end of the winding state. The power is delivered evenly via the running of the chain over a conically-shaped fusee. The function is as follows:

Barrel and fusee are connected to each other via a delicate chain consist-

The clutch paddle of the Tourbograph "Pour le Mérite" is assembled.

Tourbillon of the Tourbograph "Pour le Mérite," a steel pivoting cage consisting of eighty-four parts; the tourbillon compensates any rate inaccuracies based on gravity on the escapement system.

Inserting the tourbillon cage into the movement of the Tourbograph "Pour le Mérite."

ing of over 600 individual parts. The mechanism of the chain and fusee follows the laws of physics, in that the tension spring of a mechanical watch has different torques at the beginning and end of its winding state—particularly towards the end it has a weaker torque, which can lead to rate inaccuracies.

While winding the watch via the crown, the chain is coiled on the conically-shaped snail and the spring inside the barrel is tensioned. Then the energy is transferred via the snail—with a continuous torque—to the watch movement. The mechanism closely follows the lever principle discovered

Tourbograph "Pour le Mérite," "Homage to F.A. Lange," reference: 712.050

**Movement:** Lange manufacture caliber L903.0, manual winding. Minutes tourbillon with impulse via fusee and chain. Power reserve of 36 hours.

**Functions:** hour and minutes display, chronograph-rattrapante. Power reserve display.

**Case diameter:** 41.2 mm, honey-colored gold.

**Dial:** solid gold, argenté, guilloché.

**Hands:** blued steel and gilded.

**Glass and glass base:** sapphire glass.

**Strap:** hand-sewn croco band with honey-colored clasp.

**Limitation:** 50 units.

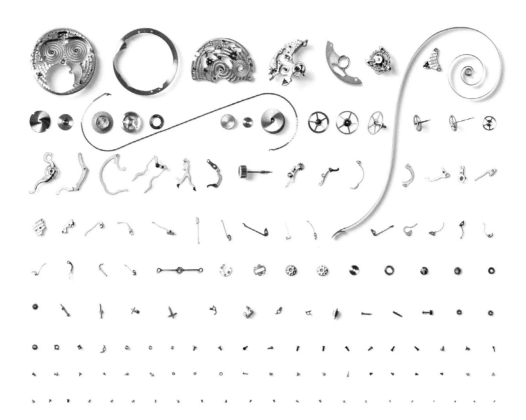

The 465 components of the Tourbograph "Pour le Mérite," Lange manufacture caliber L903.0. Manual winding, minutes tourbillon with impulse via fusee and chain, power reserve of 36 hours. The chain consists of 636 individual parts and counts as a component.

The impulse via fusee and chain of the Tourbograph "Pour le Mérite," Lange manufacture caliber L903.0. When winding the watch, a chain is uncoiled from the barrel (right) onto a cone with a circumferential winding, the snail (left).

The impulse via fusee and chain of the Tourbograph "Pour le Mérite," Lange manufacture caliber L903.0. The open barrel with the winding spring and fusee and chain enlarged. It improves the accuracy of the watch.

by Archimedes: when fully wound—that is, with a high pulling force—the chain pulls at the smaller diameter of the snail, meaning at the shorter lever, with less winding and decreasing pulling force; however, it pulls at the larger diameter of the snail and therefore at the longer lever.

But what good would it do to improve the rate precision of a watch over the entire power reserve if the watch movement stops at the precise moment when it has to be wound? For this reason a planetary gear consisting of thirty-eight parts inside

The barrel and chain are inserted into the movement of the Tourbograph "Pour le Mérite."

the snail or fusee—with only a ten-millimeter diameter—prevents this from happening and the watch movement continues to run during the winding action. It makes sure that when the movement is fully wound and the energy is at its maximum it applies force to the smaller diameter of the snail and, when the power of the mainspring diminishes, it applies force to the larger diameter of the snail and hence has an increased lever effect.

This technique, which is more effective for rate accuracy than the tourbillon,

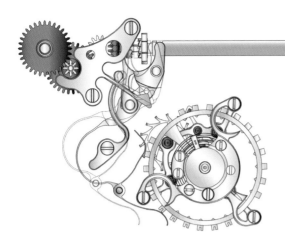

165 years - Homage to F.A. Lange Collection 2010: Tourbillon "Pour le Mérite" with the patented Lange seconds stop mechanism.

Cabaret Tourbillon, form movement caliber L042.1: illustration of the patented seconds stop mechanism for the tourbillon.

has been utilized by A. Lange & Sons since 1880. In 1994—in the first collection after the new foundation of the brand—the tourbillon "Pour le Mérite" featured this technique. With the Richard Lange "Pour le Mérite," this exclusive technology is now included in seemingly humble three-hand watches. The Kaliber L044.1, with its escapement system without a regulator, runs with 21,600 half-oscillations and has a power reserve of thirty-six hours when fully wound. The spiral of the watch is made exclusively at Lange.

In this watch, a mechanism is required that stops the watch movement before it winds down completely. This function is taken over by a converted power reserve disc that controls a stop lever. After exactly thirty-six hours the lever falls into a notch of the disc and, powered by spring pressure,

pivots via its long end into the sphere of influence of a specially shaped finger sitting on the seconds wheel axle (Sekundenradwelle), blocking it when it meets the lever. The seconds hand stays at the zero position. Finally, another construction is required to make sure that the impulse of the watch is not interrupted while winding. An elaborate planetary gear in the interior of the snail or fusee makes sure the power transmission from the snail to the watch movement is maintained while winding.

The most interesting technical details, such as the chain, the blocking mechanism, and the ratchet wheel with the fusee and the planetary gear under it, are visible through the gaps in the finely-decorated three-quarter plate. Another detail shows how far the designers have gone while pursuing precision: to optimally match the properties of the mainspring and the fusee, the thirty-six-hour working range of the mainspring can be adjusted towards a higher or lower torque via a so-called "Vorspannsperrrad" on the barrel by a service

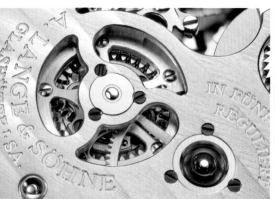

Movement of the Richard Lange "Pour le Mérite," Lange manufacture caliber L044.1, manual winding, impulse via fusee and chain, power reserve of 36 hours. Finely adjusted in five positions. Lange spiral. Seconds stop mechanism. Plates and bridges from natural nickel silver, hand-engraved balance and anchor wheel cock. Diameter: 31.6 mm. Height: 6.05 mm.

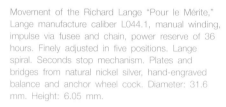

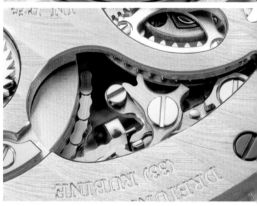

Richard Lange "Pour le Mérite," reference: 260.025
**Movement:** Lange manufacture caliber L044.1,
manual winding, impulse via fusee and chain.
Power reserve of 36 hours.
**Functions:** hour and minutes display, small
seconds with seconds stop.
**Case diameter:** 40.5 mm, platinum.
**Dial:** white enamel.
**Hands:** blued steel.
**Glass and glass base:** sapphire glass.
**Strap:** hand-sewn croco band with platinum clasp.
**Limitation:** 50 units in platinum.

watchmaker with a special tool made at Lange. A detent fastens the adjustment. The device is easily accessible on the three-quarter plate. The case is made from platinum or red gold and is 40.5 mm in diameter, helping readability. With purist clarity, the three-part enameled dial shines with narrow black Roman numerals for the hours and small red Arabic numerals for 15, 30, 45, and 60 minutes. Each of the three partial dials requires thirty lengthy operations to achieve a perfect watch dial made from enamel. The classic blued steel hands nicely contrast with the background.

Fortunately, a window showing the fusee-chain mechanism from the front was renounced.

This would not fit the character of an observation watch, where nothing should distract from knowing the precisely ascertained time at a single glance. Here A. Lange & Sons not only presents a highly precise watch, but also a piece of extraordinary artistic craft.

The dial design of the Richard Lange Tourbillon "Pour le Mérite" is based on the observation watch of Dresden master watchmaker Johann Heinrich Seyffert. For

Movement of the Tourbograph "Pour le Mérite," Lange manufacture caliber L903.0, manual winding, minutes tourbillon with impulse via fusee and chain, power reserve of 36 hours. Finely adjusted in five positions. Chronograph mechanism with rattrapante function. Plates and bridges from natural nickel silver, hand-engraved chronograph bridge.
Diameter: 30.0 mm. Heigth: 8.9 mm.

scientific observations, in those days it was often advantageous to show hours, minutes, and seconds separately to avoid confusion of the various displays, particularly under bad lighting conditions. The regulator dial provided the best conditions.

French watchmaker Louis Berthoud invented this special dial arrangement where the three time indicators are separated towards the end of the eighteenth century. Berthoud was the first to present a marine chronometer with an off-center hour hand that avoids the hour hand covering the seconds or minutes hand and therefore might prevent optimal readability. Precision pendulum clocks utilized by observatories, the post office, railways, and watch manufacturers were often fitted with a regulator dial because of its readability. A special specimen of regulator display was the precision pendulum clock by Clemens Riefler (Munich) from 1927, which also featured a twenty-four-hour display. Such large clocks are still offered today by companies like Sattler, in Munich. These clocks have a rate precision of two seconds per month and are therefore more precise than common quartz clocks.

For wristwatches, this form of time was rather unusual. Only in 1960 did the Italian Leonard Spinelli build two wristwatches with regulator dials, but it was not made as a serial production. This was done for the first time by Gerd-Rüdiger Lang twenty-seven years later with his Chronoswiss brand, featuring a three-hand watch. Today this label offers the most varied complications—tourbillon or chronograph—with regulator dial.

The so-called regulator dial usually features a central minute; small auxiliary dials are for hours and seconds. The Richard Lange Tourbillon "Pour le Mérite" differentiates itself with its three overlapping off-center dials. The three present themselves in harmonious clarity and provide the watch with an entirely new face. Its very special appeal is the fact that the gap in the dial through which the tourbillon can be observed is that of the small seconds. For the first time, a Lange watch allows viewing the chain that uncoils from the barrel when winding up until a tiny hook engages just before it is fully wound and blocks the watch movement. It is also blocked just before running out. This ensures that the spring is only tensioned in its optimal energy band. The watch features a power reserve of thirty-six hours. The traditionally hand-engraved tourbillon cock is adorned by a diamond endstone. At Lange it is only used for the most valuable movements as a marker. Another special feature is the filigree stopping mechanism which can be used to stop the movement. A timekeeper designed for supreme precision can be expected to be set to the very second. This is

taken care of by the patented stop seconds movement that Lange managed to
incorporate to stop a tourbillon. When the
filigree spring arms lower onto the tourbillon cage by pulling the crown this action
can be seen through the tourbillon window.

The Tourbillon "Pour le Mérite" in platinum
was the first Lange watch with an impulse
via fusee and chain. This watchmaking gem
was built between 1994 and 1998 in only
fifty units.

# CHRONOGRAPHS:
## *Datograph, 1815 Chronograph, Chronograph Double Split*

With respect to mechanical watches, no other model with complication has found as many enthusiasts over time as the chronograph. When French watchmaker Nicolas Rieussec presented the first chronograph in 1820, it featured a movement that placed a tiny drop of ink on the dial to mark the beginning of timekeeping.

Datograph, reference: 403.435
**Movement:** Lange manufacture caliber L951.1, manual winding. Power reserve of 36 hours.
**Functions:** hour and minutes display, small seconds with seconds stop. Chronograph with flyback and precisely jumping minutes counter. Lange large date display.
**Case diameter:** 39.0 mm, platinum.
**Dial:** solid silver, black/argenté.
Hour indexes at 3, 9, and 12 o'clock, noctilucent.
**Hands:** rhodium-plated gold and blued steel. Hour and minutes hands, noctilucent.
**Glass and glass base:** sapphire glass.
**Strap:** noble metal buckle in platinum.

Datograph, reference: 403.432
**Movement:** Lange manufacture caliber L951.1, manual winding. Power reserve of 36 hours.
**Functions:** hour and minutes display, small seconds with seconds stop. Chronograph with flyback and precisely jumping minutes counter. Lange large date display.
**Case diameter:** 39.0 mm, red gold.
**Dial:** solid silver, argenté/rhodié. Hour indexes at 3, 9, and 12 o'clock, noctilucent.
**Hands:** red gold and blued steel. Hour and minutes hands noctilucent.
**Glass and glass base:** sapphire glass.
**Strap:** noble metal buckle in red gold.

Datograph, reference: 403.035
**Movement:** Lange manufacture caliber L951.1, manual winding. Power reserve of 36 hours.
**Functions:** hour and minutes display, small seconds with seconds stop. Chronograph with flyback and precisely jumping minutes counter. Lange large date display.
**Case diameter:** 39.0 mm, platinum.
**Dial:** solid silver, black/argenté.
Hour indexes at 3, 9, and 12 o'clock, noctilucent.
**Hands:** rhodium-plated gold and blued steel. Hour and minutes hands noctilucent.
**Glass and glass base:** sapphire glass.
**Strap:** hand-sewn croco band with platinum clasp.

The first functional version of a watch with a stopping feature was developed in 1831 by Austrian Joseph Thaddäus Winnerl. His watch featured a "seconde indépendente"; that is, a mechanism that allowed for stopping and restarting the seconds hand without actually influencing the watch movement as such. This watch did not have a zero reset function. This was only realized after the invention of the Herzhebel (heart lever) in 1862 by Adolphe Nicole, who worked at the Swiss Vallée de Joux.

Here a hear-shaped disc sits on top of the tube of the seconds stop hand. While performing the zero reset, a lever

Datograph, reference: 403.032
**Movement:** Lange manufacture caliber L951.1, manual winding. Power reserve of 36 hours.
**Functions:** hour and minutes display, small seconds with seconds stop. Chronograph with flyback and presicely jumping minutes counter. Lange large date display.
**Case diameter:** 39.0 mm, red gold.
**Dial:** solid silver, argenté/rhodié. Hour indexes at 3, 9, and 12 o'clock, noctilucent.
**Hands:** red gold and blued steel. Hour and minutes hands noctilucent.
**Glass and glass base:** sapphire glass.
**Strap:** hand-sewn croco band with red gold clasp.

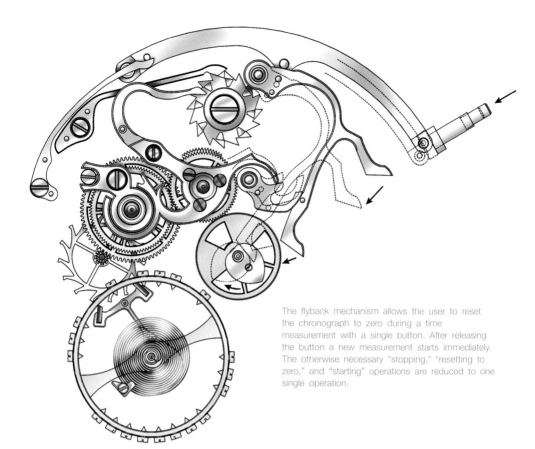

The flyback mechanism allows the user to reset the chronograph to zero during a time measurement with a single button. After releasing the button a new measurement starts immediately. The otherwise necessary "stopping," "resetting to zero," and "starting" operations are reduced to one single operation.

The dial of a Datograph is assembled.

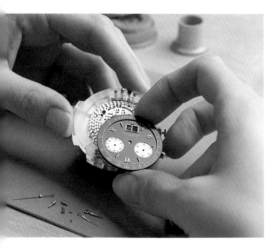

is pressed against the cam disc and puts the chronograph display into its starting position. This provided the prerequisite for the modern chronograph, which first became popular as a pocket watch and later as a single-button chronograph wristwatch. The following development of the two-button chronograph made it possible to perform cumulative split timings. An additional step towards the development of the chronograph was the quickset, where all of the running displays of the chronograph could be set to zero and

Movement of a Datograph, Lange manufacture caliber L951.1, manual winding, power reserve of 36 hours. Finely adjusted in five positions. Chronograph mechanism, flyback mechanism with precisely jumping minutes counter, patented two-disc mechanics for displaying the large date, seconds stop mechanism. Plates and bridges from natural, cross-rolled nickel silver, hand-engraved balance cock. Diameter: 30.6 mm. Height: 7.5 mm.

1815 Chronograph, reference: 402.032
**Movement:** Lange manufacture caliber L951.5, manual winding. Power reserve of 60 hours.
**Functions:** hour and minutes display, small seconds stop. Chronograph with flyback and precisely jumping minutes counter.
**Case diameter:** 39.5 mm, red gold.
**Dial:** solid silver, argenté.
**Hands:** blued steel.
**Glass and glass base:** sapphire glass.
**Strap:** hand-sewn croco band with red gold clasp.

restarted immediately. This function, also called flyback, can be found in all of the modern Lange chronographs.

With the introduction of the Datograph in 1999, Lange spontaneously established himself in the top tier of chronograph manufacturing. The watch features many traditional details that matter to the connoisseur, such as the column wheel switch, the jumping minutes, and the flyback function. The Kaliber L951.1, with its firm three-quarter plate, finely decorated bridges and plates made from nickel silver,

hand-engraved balance cock, and screwed gold chatons is also a visual sensation. Some 405 individual parts form the watch movement and allow for a precision mechanical display without peer. All of the important actions regarding function and movement can be viewed, including the stepped fusee (snail) for the precise jump of the minute hand with its patented adjustment system, the classic column wheel, and the power transmission from the basic watch movement to the chronograph movement. All of the parts are minutely finished. Wherever space

allows the screwed gold chatons set visual accents within a glamorous ambience.

Another complication of this watch is the Lange large date that characterizes the look of the watch. In conjunction with the Roman hour numerals and the circum-ferential tachymeter a sporty and classical high-end watch results.

With a power reserve of sixty hours and a proprietary Lange spiral, the 1815 Chronograph represents a successful reinterpretation of a classic watch. There is hardly any other watch in which a chronograph with the renunciation of

1815 Chronograph, reference: 402.026
**Movement:** Lange manufacture caliber L951.5,
manual winding. Power reserve of 60 hours.
**Functions:** hour and minutes display, small seconds
with seconds stop. Chronograph with flyback and
precisely jumping minutes counter.
**Case diameter:** 39.5 mm, white gold.
**Dial:** solid silver, argenté.
**Hands:** blued steel.
**Glass and glass base:** sapphire glass.
**Strap:** hand-sewn croco band with white gold clasp.

further complications has been realized in such a pure form. The dial's design picks up the display of historic pocket watches by A. Lange & Sons, with about 700 units being constructed as chronographs in those days. The two symmetrically arranged auxiliary dials for the small seconds and the thirty-minute totalizer underscore the balanced geometry of its classic look. The circumferential minute markers at the outer edge of the dial in classic "Chemin de fer"-style provide for an effortless reading of the stop time, which is precise to a fifth of a second. The precisely jumping minute counter further facilitates timekeeping.

In lively contrast to the simple elegance of its exterior, the shrewd chronograph caliber L951.5 presents a column wheel switch and stepped fusee for the precise jumping minutes. Among a wealth of mechanical refinements, a particular high point is the comfortable flyback function that can only be found on a few chronographs: with a single push of a button the 1815 Chronograph can be stopped in the middle of running timekeeping and set back. Releasing the button immediately

Double Split, reference: 404.032: movement: Lange manufacture caliber L001.1, manual winding. Power reserve of 38 hours.
**Functions:** hour and minutes display, small seconds with seconds stop. Flyback-chronograph with double rattrapante and precisely jumping minutes counter. Power reserve indicator.
**Case diameter:** 43.2 mm, red gold.

**Dial:** solid silver, argenté.
**Hands:** hour and minutes hands red gold with Superluminova; seconds and chrono hands as well as power reserve indicator and minutes counter red gold; rattrapante hand: blued steel.
**Glass and glass base:** sapphire glass.
**Strap:** hand-sewn croco band with red gold clasp.

continues the new timekeeping. A large barrel provides a considerable power reserve of sixty hours. A large eccentric balance provides rate accuracy and is powered by a balance spiral developed and manufactured in-house. It oscillates at a frequency of 18,000 half-oscillations per hour.

The sapphire glass base reveals not only one of the most technically perfect chronograph movements, but also one of the most beautiful. This glass base allows observation of most of the numerous technical and crafty fine details, such as the stepped fusee for the precisely jumping minute marker, the column wheel for steering the functions of the chronograph, or the fine adjustment of the drop-off timing via a whiplash spring on the hand-engraved balance cock.

Certainly the complexity of a chronograph movement can be increased further still by adding a second stop hand that can be independently stopped and brought to coincide with the main hand, hence the name chronograph-rattrapante. This is derived from the French verb "rattraper," meaning to jump after or run after. It is also called a split-seconds hand or a slave pointer, but these terms are not as fitting as the French equivalent; the hand is dragged along, but in contrast to other mechanisms, such as a revolution counter, it can also be brought to coincide with the main hand once again.

For the first time A. Lange & Sons has brought a genuine double-rattrapante to market with its unusual rattrapante chronograph to entice audiences and surpasses all other movements of this kind. It has not only one but two rattrapante hands—for the seconds and the minutes to be stopped—including a flyback mechanism.

This resulted in a new era of the chronograph because A. Lange & Sons has extended the "watch within a watch" by including another fascinating dimension. Until now, the delicate complication of a central rattrapante hand was regarded as the epitome of short-time measurement. This was always a highly regarded watchmaking extra with limited applications. The possibility of taking an intermediate measurement during the current measuring process via the large central rattrapante hand was limited to the sixty-second circle; that is, to the duration of a single minute. The Lange double split transferred the principle of the central rattrapante hand to the jumping minute counter. This means that for the first time the possibility of making comparative time measurements of up to thirty minutes via the classic mechanical method became a reality. This also means that the option to take intermediate time measurements did not imply a possible amplitude drop when the central chrono-hand continues

Movement of the Double Split, Lange manufacture caliber L001.1, manual winding, power reserve of 38 hours. Finely adjusted in five positions. Lange spiral. Chronograph mechanism and double rattrapante mechanism, flyback mechanism with precisely jumping minutes counter, isolator mechanism. Plates and bridges from natural cross-rolled nickel silver, hand-engraved balance cock.
Diameter: 30.6 mm. Height: 9.45 mm.

to run, which is provided by a patented isolation mechanism.

These complicated technical improvements took many years of work and development by the ateliers of the company. Inspired by the technical solutions realized by Lange towards the end of the nineteenth century—a pocket watch with a double rattrapante—Lange developed the Double Split: 220 grams of concentrated watchmaking artistry in a 43-millimeter diameter platinum case. This new milestone of watchmaking was fitted with all of the important innovations and complications developed by Lange in Glashütte, including a new balance developed in-house with eccentric adjustments instead of mass screws, providing a frequency of 21,600 half-oscillations per hour, as well as a newly developed and manufactured balance spiral of the highest quality also built in-house. It is not affixed to a stud, but to a patented spiral clamp to facilitate future adjustment processes.

All of these are detailed innovations typical of Lange, both past and present.

Double Split, reference: 404.035
**Movement:** Lange manufacture caliber L001.1, manual winding. Power reserve of 38 hours.
**Functions:** hour and minutes display, small seconds with seconds stop. Flyback-chronograph with double rattrapante and precisely jumping minutes counters. Power reserve indicator auf/ab (up/down).
**Case diameter:** 43.2 mm, platinum.
**Dial:** solid silver, black/argenté.
Hour indexes at 1, 3, 5, 7, 9, and 11 o'clock, noctilucent.
**Hands:** gold and steel. Hour and minutes hands noctilucent.
**Glass and glass base:** sapphire glass.
**Strap:** hand-sewn croco band with platinum clasp.

This is because groundbreaking work at the company's technology and development center has continued since its opening in 2003, begun by none other than Richard Lange, oldest son of the company founder Ferdinand Adolph Lange, with his patent no. 529945 for his "metal alloy for balance springs" in 1930. He discovered that the sensitivity of the spiral to temperature changes could be diminished by alloying it with beryllium, while its elasticity could be increased. Today the most modern production processes are applied at Lange—one of the world's few watch manufacturing plants—to make balance springs for its proprietary watch movements. All of this benefits the Lange Double Split, which is a unique watchmaking specialty and an exclusive item.

To comprehend such fulminant precision in all its beauty and complexity, it is best to explain its functions: the double chronograph, with its mechanical winding Kaliber L001.1 movement, is a watch that indicates on the solid silver, two-part black dial hours and minutes; on the silver-colored auxiliary dial on the left side the seconds; and below the Roman "XII," as an additional complication, the remaining power reserve. The small seconds, the opposite thirty-minute counter of the Chronograph in the silver-colored auxiliary dial, and the up and down display conform to typical Lange-style dial architecture, with its three edge points forming an equilateral triangle. While the movement of the chronograph is running, both chronograph hands can be instantly stopped by pushing the button at the four o'clock position and reset to zero. When releasing the button, the central chrono-hand—and after a minute, its minutes hand as well— start moving immediately. This so-called flyback movement makes it possible to take a new measurement without missing time. Simple chronographs required one to first push the start-stop button, then another push would reset to zero, and then yet another push of the start-stop button would restart the watch. All of these partial steps are combined with the flyback movement.

# CALENDAR AND PERPETUAL CALENDAR:

*Langematik Perpetual, Datograph Perpetual,
Saxonia Jahreskalender*

Astronomical watches—those with a calendar and moon phase display—are fascinating because of the wealth of indicators. The question arises how watchmakers are able to mechanically present such complex information in such a restricted space. In 1764, English master watchmaker Thomas Mudge was the first to present a watch with a perpetual calendar based on the calendar reform initiated by Pope Gregory XIII (1572–1585). A heretofore necessary adjustment of the calendars every three months was no longer required. The calendar reform had become necessary in the sixteenth century, as Easter was getting closer to summer. To once again coordinate the calendar with the real summer, the papal edict from March 1, 1582, determined that after October 4 of the year 1582, October 15 had to follow. To equalize future discrepancies it was decided that every four years, with a year that could be divided by four, a leap year would occur. An exception were the secular years, which are only leap years when they

Setting the hands on the dial of the Langematik Perpetual.

Assembly of the large date disc on the Langematik Perpetual.

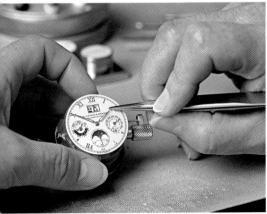

Langematik Perpetual, reference: 310.232
**Movement:** Lange manufacture caliber L922.1 Sax-0-Mat, automatic winding, rotor can be wound from both sides, power reserve of 46 hours.
**Functions:** hour and minutes display, small seconds. Hands adjustment with patented zero reset. Perpetual calendar with Lange large date, day, month, as well as four-year and leap year display. Moon phase display. Day/night indicator.
**Case diameter:** 38.5 mm, red gold.
**Dial:** solid silver, argenté.
**Hands:** red gold. Hour and minutes hands noctilucent.
**Glass and glass base:** sapphire glass.
**Strap:** noble metal clasp and buckle in red gold (left); hand-sewn croco band with red gold clasp (bottom).

are divisible by 400. This provided the Gregorian calendar with three leap years less over the course of 400 years when compared to the Julian calendar. These three leap years are not taken into account by the cadrature (mechanism to adjust the calendar) of a contemporary perpetual calendar, so it is in fact not a real perpetual calendar, as the calendar must be corrected by hand in 2100, 2200, and 2300. Nevertheless, this form of the calendar watch is preferable to that which does not require a correction with months having only thirty-one days.

Langematik Perpetual, reference: 310.025
**Movement:** Lange manufacture caliber L922.1
Sax-0-Mat, automatic winding, rotor wound from both sides, power reserve 46 hours.
**Functions:** hour and minutes display, small seconds, hands adjustment with patented zero reset. Perpetual calendar with Lange large date, day, month, as well as four-year and leap year display. Moon phase display. Day/night display.
**Case diameter:** 38.5 mm, platinum.
**Dial:** solid silver, rhodié.
**Hands:** rhodium-plated gold. Hour and minutes hands noctilucent.
**Glass and glass base:** sapphire glass.
**Strap:** hand-sewn croco band with platinum clasp.

Whether the date or the moon phase is presented as a hand or a window display varies from manufacturer to manufacturer, just like the display for leap years. This is actually obsolete, as the watch movement takes them into account anyway. The difference between a perpetual and normal calendar is the month cam, where the different lengths of the months are fixed, including an additional pivoting cam that takes into account leap years and is turned ninety degrees per year. Some perpetual calendars allow for correction of the displays via a push button set into the case, while others adjust all of the displays synchronously via the crown. A special feature at Lange is the large date in conjunction with the perpetual calendar.

In 2001, Lange was finally ready to present a perpetual calendar. The Langematik Perpetual from Glashütte was a watchmaking sensation: the world's first automatic wristwatch with perpetual calendar and large date display where the separate displays of the calendar could be corrected individually and all of them switched as a

A watchmaker assembles the Langematik Perpetual.

Assembly of the balance system of the Datograph Perpetual.

Datograph Perpetual, reference: 410.032
**Movement:** Lange manufacture caliber L952.1, manual winding. Power reserve of 36 hours.
**Functions:** hour and minutes display, small seconds with seconds stop. Chronograph with flyback and precisely jumping minutes counter. Perpetual calendar with Lange large date display, day, month, as well as four-year and leap year display. Moon phase display. Day/night display.
**Case diameter:** 41.0 mm, red gold.
**Dial:** solid silver, argenté. Noctilucent hour indexes.
**Hands:** red gold and blued steel. Noctilucent hour and minutes hands.
**Glass and glass base:** sapphire glass.
**Strap:** hand-sewn croco band with red gold clasp.

set. At first, as with the Lange 1, this was via a push button at the eleven position. Later, after some accidental operations occurred, it was via an inserted push button operated with a corrector pin. The watch was offered as a platinum and as a yellow gold version. From 2009 onward, this masterpiece of Saxon watchmaking artistry is also available with a red gold case with silver dial.

With its numerous innovations, the Langematik Perpetual is the ideal and typical interpretation of the Lange leitmotif "Tradition, state-of-the-art." At Lange, this does not mean keeping the ashes, but to pass on the fire. This watch combines the Lange tradition of the perpetual calendar founded in the second half of the nineteenth century with technical refinements that are current with the latest developments in precision watchmaking. With the unique combination of perpetual calendar, the Lange large date, the incomparable zero reset, and the main push button for the resetting by the day of all calendar indicators, with its unmatched precision it holds reference status. Once precisely adjusted the date indicator has to be reset only at the next secular year—more precisely on February 28, 2100—advancing it by one day.

Utmost precision is also a feature of the moon phase display. It deviates from the synodal lunar cycle by one day after 122.6 years of continuous runtime.

Datograph Perpetual, reference: 410.425
**Movement:** Lange manufacture caliber L952.1, manual winding. Power reserve of 36 hours.
**Functions:** hour and minutes display, small seconds with seconds stop. Chronograph with flyback and precisely jumping minutes counter. Perpetual calendar with Lange large date display, day, month as well as four-year and leap year indicator. Moon phase indicator. Day/night indicator.
**Case diameter:** 41.0 mm, platinum.
**Dial:** solid silver, rhodié.
Noctilucent hour indexes.
**Hands:** rhodium-plated gold and blued steel. Hour and minutes hands noctilucent.
**Glass and glass base:** sapphire glass.
**Strap:** noble metal buckle in platinum.

The balanced dial of the Langematik Perpetual with its Roman hour numerals appears clearly laid out and neat, despite the numerous displays: hour, minute, small seconds, additional twenty-four-hour display with day and nighttime indicator, today's date, weekday, month, leap year, and moon phase. It is characterized by prominent lanceolate hands and the Lange large date in the upper half. With an ingenious combination of flyback chronograph and a perpetual calendar, the master watchmakers at Lange once again prove their competence and skill.

While the chronographs, such as the Datograph or the Lange Double Split, allow for the measurement of very short time periods, the traditional Saxon company proved to be a "master of eternity" with the Langematik Perpetual. Its perpetual calendar has to be adjusted only at the secular year 2100—a leap year according to the Gregorian calendar—with one single push of a button. With the Datograph

Datograph Perpetual, reference: 410.030
**Movement:** Lange manufacture caliber L952.1, manual winding. Power reserve of 36 hours.
**Functions:** hour and minutes display, small seconds with seconds stop. Chronograph with flyback and precisely jumping minutes counter. Perpetual calendar with Lange large date display, day, month as well as four-year and leap year display. Moon phase display. Day/night display.
**Case diameter:** 41.0 mm, white gold.
**Dial:** solid silver, grey. Noctilucent hour indexes.
**Hands:** rhodium-plated gold and blued steel. Hour and minutes hands noctilucent.
**Glass and glass base:** sapphire glass.
**Strap:** hand-sewn croco band with white gold clasp.

Movement of the Datograph Perpetual, Lange manufacture caliber L952.1, manual winding, power reserve of 36 hours. Finely adjusted in five positions. Lange spiral. Chronograph mechanism, flyback mechanism with precisely jumping minutes counter, patented two-disc mechanism for displaying the large date; calendar mechanism with day, month, four-year and leap year display, seconds stop mechanism. Plates and bridges from natural nickel silver, hand-engraved balance cock. Diameter: 32.0 mm. Height: 8.0 mm.

Perpetual, the most outstanding innovations of these two watch types are combined into a watch of superlatives. For the second time, the Lange large date becomes an "eternal large date" and, combined with the newly developed perpetual calendar, overcomes the irregularities of the perpetual calendar. The correct date is always displayed, including leap years.

Apart from the weekday, month, and the four-year cycle with the leap year and the moon phase, the new Lange watch also displays daytime/nighttime change. Due to the high precision of its mechanics, the moon phase deviates only a single day from the actual lunar orbit after 122 years.

But the Datograph Perpetual proves its particular excellency not only with regards to the long time periods it measures. It is also a specialist of short time measurements and expands its already considerable capabilities with the useful functions of the legendary Lange chronographs: flyback, jumping minute counter, and column wheel switch. This allows determining time down to a fifth of a second. The complex movement of the Datograph Perpetual consists of 556 parts of the highest quality and mostly decorated by hand. Lange has purposefully expanded its catalog of watches with important complications while at the same time remaining faithful to its long tradition of building perfectly simple and extremely complicated masterpieces.

The Datograph Perpetual features a sapphire glass base, allowing view of the movement of the exclusive Kaliber L952.1 manual winding mechanism with its bridges and plates in natural nickel silver. This is also true for the very small but decisive parts that only very few companies are able to manufacture themselves, such as the balance's coiled spring. The Datograph Perpetual is fitted with a newly developed balance spring optimized for this type of watch and is entirely manufactured in-house. It provides the watch movement running at 2.5 Hertz—equivalent to 18,000 balance half-oscillations per hour—with optimal rate accuracy. This is also due to the contribution of the glucydur balance developed by Lange with adjustment regulating cams. Additionally, a special cog wheel barrel case allows only those tension states of the tension spring to be effective that provide for a near constant torque, contributing to the rate accuracy. The Lange designers developed a new switching mechanism for the perpetual calendar. By using teeth of different lengths and a special shape of the cover at the calendar switch disc only one pawl. This arrangement,

registered for patent approval in March 2005, requires a shorter switching distance when manually setting the calendar and allows for smooth switching of the large date. The complex calendar mechanism consists of 223 parts that only contribute 1.9 mm to the total height of the watch (13.5 mm). It is autonomous until the leap year of the Gregorian calendar in 2100 and requires only one additional correction in 2200.

The calendar display can not only be individually set with a recessed button; the Datograph Perpetual features a practical universal corrector, allowing for synchronized setting of all of the calendar displays— including the date—either at the same time or day-by-day. So this does not occur accidentally, this operation requires pulling the crown.

The new exceptional watch by Lange whose construction requires several months certainly exhibits its special status inside its platinum case. With a case diameter of forty-one mm, it is one of the Lange large-format watches. The solid silver dial with rhodium-plated gold appliqués provides visual restraint and a high level of clarity. The hands of the time indicators are noctilucent thanks to Superluminova — beauty and practical aspects once again create a harmonious combination. If the perpetual calendar is too expensive for you but you do not want to forego precise

Datograph Perpetual, reference: 410.025
**Movement:** Lange manufacture caliber L952.1, manual winding. Power reserve of 36 hours.
**Functions:** hour and minutes display, small seconds with seconds stop. Chronograph with flyback and precisely jumping minutes counter. Perpetual calendar with Lange large date display, day, month as well as four-year and leap year display. Moon phase display. Day/night display.
**Case diameter:** 41.0 mm, platinum.
**Dial:** solid silver, rhodié. Noctilucent hour indexes.
**Hands:** rhodium-plated gold and blued steel. Hour and minutes hands noctilucent.
**Glass and glass base:** sapphire glas.
Band: hand-sewn croco band with platinum clasp.

Mounting the large date disc onto the Langematik Perpetual.

calendar indications, Lange now offers a yearly calendar that only has to be reset in February. In the Saxonia Jahreskalender (yearly calendar), the watchmaking complication with the greatest practical value in daily life is now available for the first time in a Lange watch. Below its dial, with its appealing clear design, an elaborate mechanical program automatically shows the day of the week, date, and the month, taking into account their varying lengths. The calendar has to be corrected only once per year. The three calendar displays and the moon phase present themselves on the dial with exemplary clarity.

With this new watch in the elegant Saxonia style, A. Lange & Sons follows its great tradition in a modern way and has continuously brought forth watchmaking milestones. Apart from the unique combination of the yearly calendar with the typical Lange large date, the Saxonia Jahreskalender features an extremely precise moon phase indicator, as well as the famous Sax-0-Mat-Automatikkaliber and its sophisticated zero reset mechanism.

With its superior features, this watch has everything it takes to become the reference of this watchmaking calendar discipline. During the development of the Saxonia Jahreskalender, Lange's product designers applied extreme care for both a clear and aesthetically balanced arrangement of the displays on the dial. With its dagger-shaped hands, its restrained minute markers, and the rhombically arranged calendar displays, the dial appears refreshingly clear. It is characterized by prominent lanceolate hands and, in the upper half, by the easily readable Lange large date with its characteristic double window. This is based on a modern design principle of gaining beauty from functionality. The most important information, such as time and date, are available at first sight. The second veers towards the left, to the auxiliary dial at nine o'clock that displays the day of the week. At six o'clock the moon makes its appearance. The same location shows the elaborate inner life with small seconds. The auxiliary dial at three o'clock is reserved for the months. The calendar of the Saxonia Jahreskalender sets the months with thirty and thirty-one days all by itself and only once a year, during the transition of the last day of February to the first day of May, does it require adjustment.

After a prolonged period of wearing the watch all three calendar displays and the moon phase can be quickly and individually set via a recessed button.

The foundation for this exclusive movement consists of one of the most modern and elaborate automatic move-

Saxonia Jahreskalender (yearly calendar), reference: 330.032
**Movement:** Lange manufacture caliber L085.1, automatic winding, rotor wound from both sides. Power reserve of 46 hours.
**Functions:** hour and minutes display, small seconds. Patented zero reseet, yearly calendar with Lange large date, day, month and moon phase display.
**Case diameter:** 38.5 mm, red gold.
**Dial:** solid silver, argenté.
**Hands:** red gold and blued steel.
**Glass and glass base:** sapphire glass.
**Strap:** hand-sewn croco band with red gold clasp.

ments: the Sax-0-Mat-Kaliber, finished with the highest precision and awarded several times over. The zero at the center of its name indicates the patented zero reset function that stops the watch movement when pulling the crown and conveniently resets the seconds hand to zero for setting time with utmost precision. The movement is also technically unique due to the construction of its winding mechanism: the ball bearing mounted golden rotor with additional platinum flywheel mass winds up the watch from both sides. Even in the case of a casual wearer there is always sufficient power reserve being created.

Much passion and time is spent at Lange with the finissage of parts. Even surfaces which will not be visible later on feature elaborate ribbings and polishings. The hand-engraved balance cock turns each watch into a unicum. The Saxonia Jahreskalender is available with a white or red gold 38.5 mm diameter case.

Saxonia Jahreskalender (yearly calendar), reference: 330.026

**Movement:** Lange manufacture caliber L085.1, automatic winding, rotor wound from both sides. Power reserve of 46 hours.

**Functions:** hour and minutes display, small seconds. Patented zero reset, yearly calendar with Lange large date, day, month and moon phase display.

**Case diameter:** 38.5 mm, white gold.

**Dial:** blued steel

**Glass and glass base:** sapphire glass.

**Strap:** hand-sewn croco band with white gold clasp.

# WORLD TIME WATCH:
## Lange 1 Zeitzone (time zone)

If you follow a sundial, you will notice that twelve noon differs considerably even within short geographic distances, as the sun travels east to west and time follows along. In eras when the stagecoach was the fastest means of land transportation this was tolerable, but with the increasing prominence of railway transportation starting in 1860, the coordination of rapidly flowing traffic without a standard time was increasingly difficult. Around 1850, there were 144 recognized times in the US; even thirty years later there were still eighty. No wonder even early pocket watches offered multiple time displays to find one's way in a world of inflationary time. Scotsman Sandford Fleming pressed for an international conference in October 1884, with twenty-four sovereign states participating. At this "International Meridian Conference," Fleming suggested to divide the 360 degrees of the earth by the twenty-four hours in a day. Every fifteen degrees of longitude the same time should be valid, with an offset of one hour from longitude to longitude. The zero meridian ran through the Greenwich observatory—back then a small town and now a district of London. The antimeridian is located in the Pacific, between Samoa and Auckland. GMT therefore simply means

Greenwich Mean Time. At the same time, there was an agreement to divide the day into twenty-four hours. The Americans were the exception, who left it at twelve hours, requiring the addition of noon (a.m. = ante meridian) and after noon (p.m. = post meridian).

After 1919, an internationally accepted world time was introduced—the "Universal Time Coordinated," or UTC—where a four-digit number allowed setting an exact time across continents.

Watches with time zones already existed in the eighteenth century. Even today watches with a second or third time zone, including world time watches that feature a ring of cities for determining the corresponding local time, are an attractive complication, particularly for frequent flyers.

Even if you are only globally active on the phone this type of watch is helpful. Once you have awakened a business partner at three in the morning you will then first glance at the GMT or a world time watch before calling again. The problem of time zones is still cause for irritation.

Hence, the Lange 1 Zeitzone follows both a simple and practical principle: either the home time has priority on the larger of the off-center dials, in which case a

Rear view: movement of the Lange 1 Zeitzone (time zone), Lange manufacture caliber L031.1, manual winding, power reserve of 72 hours. Finely adjusted in five positions. Double barrel, patented two-disc mechanics for displaying the large date, seconds stop mechanism, 67-part adjustment and corrective mechanism for zone time and city ring. Plates and bridges from natural nickel silver, hand-engraved balance cock and intermediate wheel cock. Diameter: 34.1 mm. Height: 6.65 mm.

second pair of hands easily set with a push button and a pivoting city ring displays a second time zone on a small auxiliary dial reserved for the seconds display for the Lange 1; or, a cleverly constructed adjustment mechanism provides the option—whenever any time zone should become the new "home time"—to reverse the priority of the two time displays. The time at the new location becomes the new home time and includes the date function, while the auxiliary dial displays either the correct home time or any other time zone, entirely dependent on the user's preference. The owner of this watch has limitless possibilities to handle all of the world's time zones with ease. The freedom of an all-encompassing mobility must conform to the astronomical conditions both mechanically and with respect to watchmaking, in that the earth rotates around its axis once every twenty-four hours, facing the sun and then turning away, resulting in the days and nights starting and ending at different times within the twenty-four time zones. This watch's separate and synchronized day and night display for the two adjustable time zones is thus a very useful function. The Lange 1 Zeitzone displays the day and night phase for the home time and the second synchronizable time via the city ring with small arrow hands and a dark-light marking. This method allows for practical use of the second time zone. Even if you only talk on the phone worldwide, you need to know at what time you might be reaching a partner at the other end of the world.

Let us consider a normal use of the user-friendly construction that the Lange 1 Zeitzone features: a voyage around the world, whether by plane or only in your mind, starts with this Lange watch by pushing the button at the eight o'clock position. This corrector not only switches

Lange 1 Zeitzone (time zone), reference: 116.033
**Movement:** Lange manufacture caliber L031.1, manual winding. Power reserve of 72 hours.
**Functions:** asymmetric hour and minutes display, small seconds with seconds stop, Lange large date. Zone time with city ring. Separate day/night displays for main and zone time, power reserve display auf/ab (up/down).
**Case diameter:** 41.9 mm, red gold.
**Dial:** red gold.
**Glass and glass base:** sapphire glass.
**Strap:** hand-sewn croco band with red gold clasp.

Lange 1 Zeitzone (time zone), reference: 116.025 asia

**Movement:** Lange manufacture caliber L031.1, manual winding. Power reserve of 72 hours.
**Functions:** asymmetric hour and minutes display, small seconds with seconds stop, Lange large date display. Zone time with city ring. Separate day/night display for main and zone time, power reserve display auf/ab (up/down), version with Singapore on the city ring.
**Case diameter:** 41.9 mm, platinum.
**Dial:** solid silver, rhodié.
**Hands:** rhodium-plated gold and blued steel.
**Glass and glass base:** sapphire glass.
**Strap:** hand-sewn croco band with platinum clasp.

the pivoting city ring at the edge of the dial one time zone, in one-hour steps—when seen geographically—towards the east, but also the hour hand of the time zone, which is then automatically synchronized at any moment with the display of the city ring.

A small appliqué arrow on the dial of the time zone at five o'clock—closest to the city ring—is the reference point for setting a second time. After twenty-four adjustment steps, the earth has been circumnavigated once in time. The numerals for the time zone are Arabic, as opposed to the gold-colored Roman appliqués of the home time.

In case of a longer stay in a location, the watch offers a technologically unique solution. The display of the main time, including the function of the patented large date, can be converted to the real "home time." The outer city ring and an adjustment mechanism come in handy, using the crown—with a depressed time zone correction button—to set the heretofore home time of the large dial to the new local time. This adjustment operation causes the hour hand of the time zone to stop. It allows for redefining and setting the new main time for any location in the world—if necessary, including a simple date correction via the date correction button. In each case, both time displays correctly inform whether it is day or night at the

Lange 1 Zeitzone, reference: 116.025
**Movement:** Lange manufacture caliber L031.1,
manual winding. Power reserve of 72 hours.
**Functions:** asymmetric hour and minutes display,
small seconds with seconds stop, Lange large
date display. Zone time with city ring. Separate
day/night display for main and zone time, power
reserve indicator auf/ab (up/down).
**Case diameter:** 41.9 mm, platinum.
**Dial:** solid silver, rhodié.
**Hands:** rhodium-plated gold and blued steel.
**Glass and glass base:** sapphire glass.
**Strap:** hand-sewn croco band with platinum clasp.

Lange 1 Zeitzone (time zone), reference: 116.021asia
**Movement:** Lange manufacture caliber L031.1,
manual winding. Power reserve of 72 hours.
**Functions:** asymmetric hour and minutes display,
small seconds with seconds stop, Lange large date
display. Zone time with city ring. Separate day/night
displays for main and zone time, power reserve
indicator auf/ab (up/down), version with Singapore
inside of the city ring.
**Case diameter:** 41.9 mm, yellow gold.
**Dial:** solid silver, champagne.
**Hands:** yellow gold and blued steel.
**Glass and glass base:** sapphire glass.
**Strap:** hand-sewn croco band with yellow gold clasp.

current location and at home. Experience has shown that only unambiguous watch systems for a second time zone are practical, and the Lange 1 Zeitzone and its two adjustment methods have ingeniously solved this issue.

The watch, with the Lange manual winding caliber L031.1, certainly features all of the advantages of the Lange 1, such as over three days of power reserve thanks to its double mainspring barrel, four screwed gold chatons, the screw balance with whiplash precision index adjuster, and the hand-engraved balance cock. The gears for running the time zone lie on top of the three-quarter plate and are visible through the sapphire glass base. The required intermediate-wheel cock also features the distinctive appearance of the master engravers at Lange. Two additional complications are the patented large date and the power reserve indicator at three o'clock.

Lange 1 Zeitzone, reference: 116.021
**Movement:** Lange manufacture caliber L031.1, manual winding. Power reserve of 72 hours.
**Functions:** asymmetric hour and minutes display, small seconds with seconds stop, Lange large date display. Zone time with city ring. Separate day/night display for main and zone time, power reserve display auf/ab (up/down).
**Case diameter:** 41.9 mm, yellow gold.
**Dial:** solid silver, champagne.
**Hands:** yellow gold and blued steel.
**Glass and glass base:** sapphire glass.
**Strap:** hand-sewn croco band with yellow gold clasp.

# MOON PHASE:

*Lange 1 Mondphase, Cabaret Mondphase,*
*Grosse Lange 1 "Luna Mundi" (2003-2004),*
*1815 Mondphase (1999-2000)*

There is hardly another attribute that causes similar astonishment at first sight than the moon phase. The small moon, which apparently moves synchronized with our heavenly companion inside a window, constitutes an astronomical display that is still meaningful for many of us. Some people set their activities to the moon: a visit to the hairdresser or a pending operation is only done with a waxing moon; and many friends that garden swear by the particular moon phases for sowing and harvesting.

Today, this is sometimes perceived as superstition, but this custom has a religious and sociohistorical background dating from ancient times: the Chinese, Egyptians, Babylonians, and Indians revered the sun and moon just like the Incas and Mayas as a sign of the world changing continuously to the rhythm of the celestial bodies. The most visible and easiest

Movement of the Lange 1 Mondphase (moon phase), Lange manufacture caliber L901.5, manual winding, power reserve of 72 hours. Finely adjusted in five positions. Double barrel, patented two-disc mechanism for displaying the large date, seconds stop mechanism, Lange moon disc. Plates and bridges from natural nickel silver, hand-engraved balance cock. Diameter: 30.4 mm. Height: 5.9 mm.

Kleine Lange 1 Mondphase (small moon phase), reference: 819.049

**Movement:** Lange manufacture caliber L901.9. Manual winding. Power reserve of 72 hours.

**Functions:** hour and minutes display, small seconds with seconds stop, moon phase display, Lange large date display, power reserve indicator auf/ab (up/down).

**Case diameter:** 36.8 mm, white gold.

**Dial:** solid silver, dark blue, covered with natural mother-of-pearl.

**Hands:** rhodium-plated gold.

**Glass and glass base:** sapphire glass.

**Strap:** hand-sewn ray leather band with white gold clasp.

**Limitation:** 150 units.

141

Movement of the 1815 Mondphase (moon phase) from the "165 Years - Homage to F.A. Lange Collection 2010." Lange manufacture caliber L961.2, manual winding, power reserve of 45 hours. Finely adjusted in five positions. Time display with hour, minutes, small seconds with seconds stop. Precisely calculated moon phase to 1,058 years. Lange spiral. Plates and bridges from natural nickel silver, three-quarter plates with ray grind. Balance cock from honey-colored gold, hand-engraved.
Diameter: 27.5 mm. Height: 3.85 mm.

celestial object to follow its movement is the moon. New moon, waxing moon, and waning moon are phases that allow for organizing the month. This celestial body, depending on its position on its elliptic trajectory, is between 225,558 and 252,276 miles from the earth and requires twenty-seven days, forty-three minutes, and twelve seconds for one earth orbit. The fact that one lunation takes twenty-nine days, twelve hours, forty-four minutes, and 2.8 seconds is caused by the additional movement of the earth around the sun. In a watch, a moon phase is rounded to twenty-nine days and twelve hours. Since fifty-nine days can be better displayed mechanically than half that, two moons are featured on the moon phase display, so sooner or later the display must be adjusted manually.

At Lange, this problem was solved with a continuously running display, so that only 1.9 seconds per month are lost and an adjustment of the moon phase display is necessary after 122 years. Furthermore, the moon's movement in the northern and southern hemispheres is reversed. Lange found an original solution for this as well with the "Luna Mundi" as the "Southern Cross" in red gold with brown croco leather strap and as an "Ursa Major" in white gold with black croco leather strap displaying the moon phases of both hemispheres correctly. The moon phase disc also displays the constellation of Ursa Major or the Southern Cross. For the display of the southern hemisphere, an additional idle wheel had to be added that reverses the direction of the moon phase display.

This flagship of A. Lange & Sons also features a realistic moon phase display. The Lange 1 Mondphase is an additional complication for this series next to the large date, power reserve display, day display, and even tourbillon. Usually a disc with fifty-nine teeth is used for the moon phase display, resulting in a rounded moon cycle of 29.5 days with a deviation of forty-four minutes and three seconds. Over the course of two and a half years this amounts to a full day. Furthermore, this type of construction, where the moon disc is not switched continuously but only once or twice a day, creates a deviation of the display of more than six and, respectively, three degrees before the switching process.

The much more elaborate movement of the Lange 1 Mondphase not only moves the moon phase display continuously and therefore congruent with the synodal moon, but it minimizes the mechanically inevitable display error to only 1.9 seconds per day, or fifty-seven seconds per moon orbit; in mathematical terms, this is a deviation of only 0.002 percent. This results in a deviation of only one day over the course of 122.6 years. With the button inserted into the case between the seven and eight

The Cabaret with moon phase display was the first complication of this series, apart from the large date and the tourbillon as the crowning glory.

143

Lange 1 Mondphase (moon phase), reference: 109.032
**Movement:** Lange manufacture caliber L901.5, manual winding. Power reserve of 72 hours.
**Functions:** asymmetric hour and minutes display, small seconds with seconds stop, moon phase display, Lange large date display, power reserve auf/ab (up/down).
**Case diameter:** 38.5 mm, red gold.
**Dial:** solid silver, argenté.
**Hands:** red gold.
**Glass and glass base:** sapphire glass.
**Strap:** hand-sewn croco band with red gold clasp.

o'clock positions, deviations can be corrected seemlessly at any time. Furthermore, the moon phase display can be adjusted again after the watch has not been used for an extended period of time.

Part of the quality features of the further developed Kaliber L901.5 manual winding mechanism—consisting of 398 individual parts—is the robust Glashütte plate from cross-rolled nickel silver, the double barrel for a power reserve of over three days, the patented Lange large date, the hand-engraved balance cock with whiplash precision index adjuster and a shockproof screw balance with 21,600 half-oscillations per hour, stop seconds, fifty-four jewels—nine of them in screwed gold chatons—hand-blued screws, hand-beveled and polished plate edges, the Glashütte ribbing or sunburst polishing on plates and bridges, and an endstone set into a gold chaton on a separate anchor disc cock supported by a classic black-polished steel platelet.

The Lange 1 Mondphase is available in three cases with hand-sewn croco leather straps, as well as with the sturdy Lange pin buckle: yellow gold (model no. 109.021), red gold (model no. 109.032), and platinum (model no. 109.025). Straps and clasps made from precious metals can be custom-ordered, as is the case with most Lange watches. The solid three-part cases with sapphire glass and sapphire glass base feature the button for quick adjustment of the Lange large date at the left upper case edge at ten o'clock, and between seven and eight o'clock the button for the moon phase display inserted into the case. The non-slip crown with the embossed Lange logo shows perfection down to the last detail: it is used for winding the watch movement and for precisely setting the watch. The displays on the asymmetric and stepped dial made from solid silver show hours, minutes, seconds, power reserve, and large date, and now include the moon phase display inside of the seconds circle, harmoniously located in a strict and neat arrangement.

The Lange 1 Mondphase also reflects the magic of the night with its luminous main hand, including the power reserve indicator as well as the luminous hour indexes. This, and the delicately worked dials from solid silver with their raised hour and minute circle, emphasize the special character of this Lange 1, which promises a new aesthetic and technical treat for enthusiasts of ultimate watchmaking artistry. In this case, the asymmetric dial architecture designed in 1990 for the first Lange watch of the modern era has proven to be a long-term decision: the position of the moon phase display on the dial corresponds to the most important display—the hour and minutes circle of the watch—just as the positions of the moon to the earth.

Lange 1 Mondphase (moon phase), reference: 109.025
**Movement:** Lange manufacture caliber L901.5, manual winding. Power reserve of 72 hours.
**Functions:** asymmetric hour and minutes display, small seconds with seconds stop, moon phase display, Lange large date display, power reserve indicator auf/ab (up/down).
**Case diameter:** 38.5 mm, platinum.
**Dial:** solid silver, rhodié.
**Hands:** rhodium-plated gold.
**Glass and glass base:** sapphire glass.
**Strap:** hand-sewn croco band with platinum clasp.

Another mechanical winding movement watch with moon phase—this time rectangular—is the Cabaret. It is the stylistic caprice among the Lange watches. Everything that distinguishes an A. Lange & Son watch is perfectly featured here, such as the time display with golden hands and appliqués. Or the large date, which has a surprising effect on the rectangular dial, as its user-friendly size seems to contradict its small dimensions. The patented two-disc mechanics hidden behind this small gem have solved this problem ten years ago in an elegant fashion, and it has also inspired the watchmaking industry regarding date displays.

As a visual counterpoint, the striking seconds display of the Cabaret has played a somewhat pert yet harmonizing role within the stylistic ensemble, sharing its appearance with the new Cabaret Mondphase, with a classic moon phase display. The small new moon theater with the rising and falling of earth's companion is a real enrichment and almost a must for night owls or friends of the moon. Behind the scenes, the Cabaret offers quite a lot, and the Kaliber L931.5 watch movement allows for deep insight into the quality philosophy of Lange behind the glass: three-quarter plate from natural nickel silver, a Glashütte serrated bevel with blued screws, screw balance with whiplash precision index adjuster, and a hand-en-graved balance cock where a master engraver places the artistic logo on all Lange watches. The manual winding mechanism of the Cabaret Mondphase features forty-one hours of power reserve when fully wound.

The switching of the additional integrated moon phase mechanism occurs automatically once per day between 17:00 and 19:00. However, the moon can also be set via a laterally inserted button in case the watch has not been worn for some time, or if the mechanical deviation of the moon disc which completes two moon orbits per turn with its two moons and fifty-nine teeth sums up one day of deviation. This will be the case every thirty-two months, as the synodal orbital duration of the moon is not precisely twenty-nine, but 29.5306 days.

As is the case with calendar watches or perpetual calendars, moon phase watches are also difficult and unnerving to reset once they have stopped. With automatic watches the watchwinder is adequate to prevent them from stopping. For manual watches, the Orbita company offers a device that winds up the watch daily via the winding crown. A microprocessor continuously measures the resistance of the spring and controls the winding process. However, such a device is not exactly cheap and costs several times as much as a normal watchwinder.

The Grosse Lange 1 Luna Mundi (41.9 mm
diameter) "Southern Cross" (left) and "Ursa Major."
The former displays the correct moon phase of
the southern hemisphere, the white gold version
that of the northern. Both could only be
purchased as a set.

1815 Mondphase (moon phase) "Homage to F.A. Lange," reference: 212.050

**Movement:** Lange manufacture caliber L943.2, manual winding. Power reserve of 45 hours.
**Functions:** hour and minutes display, small seconds with seconds stop. Moon phase calculated precisely to 1,058 years. Lange spiral.
**Case diameter:** 37.4 mm, honey-colored gold.
**Dial:** solid gold, argenté, guilloché.
**Hands:** blued steel.
**Glass and glass base:** sapphire glass.
**Strap:** hand-sewn croco band with honey-colored gold clasp.
**Limitation:** 265 units.

Early in the history of the mechanical watch, the moon phase became a popular complication and more and more people were enthralled by the wandering moon disc on the dial. As early as 1650, a pocket watch by Belgian Heinrich Verstylen with moon phase and calendar display was available, proving that people have been enjoying this complication for over 350 years.

# JUMPING TIME DISPLAY:
## *Lange Zeitwerk, Grosse Lange 1 "Luminous"*

Compared to traditional Lange watches, the Lange "Luminous" model utilizes a completely new form language: the nickel silver time bridge stretches over the entire width of the dial to prominently frame the large numerals of the adjacent hour and minutes display. Towards the bottom it encloses the auxiliary dial of the small seconds and unites the three units of time measurement into a harmonious whole. The crown, with its beveled knurling, is grippy and points to the upper right, which is rather unconventional. The top third features the remaining power reserve and reliably informs when it is time to add fresh energy to the movement.

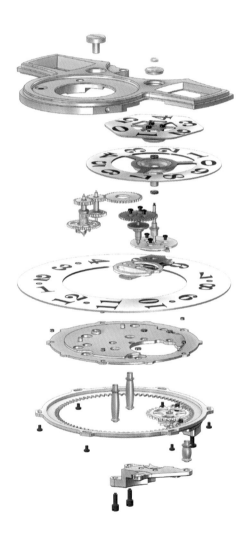

Jumping numerals mechanism of the Lange Zeitwerk (timeworks). The manufacture caliber L043.1 features an entirely new jumping numerals mechanism for hours and minutes. The construction follows the Lange principle, consisting of two minutes discs and a large hour ring. At precisely every full minute a constant-force escapement provides the required switching impulse. When viewed from the glass base side, the movement presents a large number of additional future-oriented inventions.

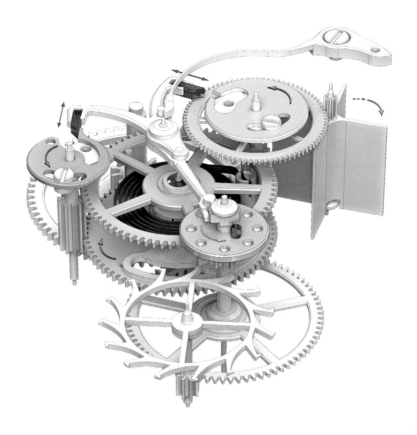

The watch with the programmatic name Lange Zeitwerk (timework) stands for uncompromising clarity, as it clearly displays the current time with a heretofore unavailable digital mechanical display size: with a gentle click and without delay the minutes display switches from one minute to the next in a fraction of a second, until the watch makes the big jump towards the full hour and all three numeral discs switch forward one step. Here, time becomes an event; 11:59 is the perfect moment for the showdown *High Noon* in widescreen format. The eye is spellbound, following the leisurely progressing analog display of

Constant-force escapement of the Lange Zeitwerk, Lange manufacture caliber L043.1. A constant-force escapement is mounted between the barrel disc and the balance. This patented construction fulfills two important functions. It provides the energy for the jumping switching of the hour and minutes display. It picks up the principle known from large clocks regarding the striking mechanism principle with warning and decreasing resolution, and as such it is unique in this size. On the other hand, the constant-force escapement ensures that the balance receives an almost totally constant impulse over the entire runtime, contributing to rate accuracy.

Dial and rear view of the movement of the Lange Zeitwerk, Lange manufacture caliber L043.1, manual winding, power reserve of 36 hours. Finely adjusted in five positions. Innovative jumping numerals mechanism. Constant-force escapement provides the impulse for the jumping dial and for a controlled torque delivery. Patented barrel construction. Plates and bridges from natural nickel silver, hand-engraved balance cock.
Diameter: 33.6 mm. Height: 9.25 mm.

the small seconds. Time seems to be going slower the more you pay attention to it. Thirty seconds to go—the tension slowly increases. Then it is ten, three, two, one—click—and the digital mechanical display jumps to 12:00.

The new look is matched on the inside of the 41.9-mm gold or platinum case by a fitting and trend-setting movement that takes advantage of the available space with a 33.6 mm diameter. The high energy requirement for switching the three time discs at the full hour in a synchronized way is supplied by its newly developed barrel with a sturdy winding spring. Its patented construction literally turns the well-known winding method on its head. As such, the bearing of the barrel, which

has more friction, is always used when the watch is wound up, while the barrel disc pivots inside of the bearing with less friction when the watch unwinds. This provides increased torque for the drive of the watch and the disc mechanics of the time display.

Between barrel and balance a patented constant-force escapement acts as a pacemaker for the jumping switch of the hour and minutes display. A fan propeller was integrated into the construction to absorb the extraordinarily large forces resulting from the acceleration and braking of the numeral discs. The air resistance that counters its rotation absorbs a significant amount of energy and makes for smooth switching operations. At the same time, the constant-force escapement provides an important contribution to the rate accuracy, ensuring that the watch is powered with close to constant force during its entire thirty-six-hour power reserve—independent of the winding state of the watch and without influence of the energy-consuming switching operations occurring every minute. The precise clock generator of the watch consists of an eccentric balance with a balance spring manufactured in-house.

With all of its progressiveness, this watch continues to advocate classic watchmaking values: the view through the sapphire glass bottom reveals the elaborately

Lange Zeitwerk, reference: 140.032
**Movement:** Lange manufacture caliber L043.1, manual winding. Power reserveof 36 hours.
**Functions:** hour and minutes as jumping numerals display, small seconds with seconds stop. Power reserve indicator auf/ab (up/down).
**Case diameter:** 41.9 mm, red gold.
**Dial:** solid silver, argenté.
**Time bridge:** natural nickel silver.
**Hands:** red gold.
**Glass and glass base:** sapphire glass.
**Strap:** hand-sewn croco band with red gold clasp.

Lange Zeitwerk (timeworks), reference: 140.029
**Movement:** Lange manufacture caliber L043.1, manual winding. Power reserve of 36 hours.
**Functions:** hour and minutes as jumping numerals display, small seconds with seconds stop. Power reserve indicator auf/ab (up/down).

**Case diameter:** 41.9 mm, white gold.
**Dial:** solid silver, black.
**Time bridge:** rhodium-plated gold.
**Glass and glass base:** sapphire glass.
**Strap:** hand-sewn croco band with white gold clasp.

Lange Zeitwerk "Luminous", reference: 140.035
**Movement:** Lange manufacture caliber L043.3, manual winding. Power reserve of 36 hours.
**Functions:** hour and minutes as jumping numerals display, small seconds with seconds stop. Power reserve indicator auf/ab (up/down).
**Case diameter:** 41.9 mm, platinum.

**Dial:** PVD-coated sapphire glass.
**Time bridge:** rhodium-plated nickel silver.
**Hands:** rhodium-plated gold.
**Glass and glass base:** sapphire glass.
**Strap:** hand-sewn croco band with platinum clasp.
**Limitation:** 100 units in platinum.

155

decorated Manufactured caliber L043.1 which, apart from all of its technological updates, features the three-quarter plate, hand-engraved balance cock, and screwed gold chatons—the familiar and noble foundation of every Lange watch. With its outer appearance and interior values, the Lange Zeitwerk is a reinterpretation of classic watchmaking artistry. Traditionalists might be stunned, but they should consider that digital mechanical displays have a long history in watchmaking and are not a modern invention.

The Luminous variation of the Zeitwerk watch presents an innovation, as it allows reading of the its display in complete darkness. Conventional noctilucent watches with phosphorescent hands and indexes are charged by daylight. The numerals of the Lange Zeitwerk are hidden inside the dial and in the dark most of the time. To be luminous at night, the task was to

guide sunlight into the interior of the watch, so the solid silver dial was replaced with a semi-transparent one, creating the reverse effect of sunglasses.

However, complete transparency would allow an unobstructed view of the interior and would compromise the unique clarity of the display. The designers at Lange took advantage of the principle where the phosphorescent coating of the numerals is provided particularly by energy-rich UV rays. Hence, the sapphire glass is coated with a substance that allows UV rays to pass through but mostly blocks the visible light spectrum—contrary to sunglasses, which block UV rays while letting the visible light pass through. When watching more closely, the three discs with numerals can barely be noticed, and this provides the watch its unique appearance.

# THE FIRST STRIKING WATCH WITH DIGITAL TIME DISPLAY:
## Lange Zeitwerk "Striking Time"

The Lange Zeitwerk Striking Time is the world's first mechanical wristwatch with a jumping numerals display featuring an integrated visible striking mechanism. It plays the famous main theme from Beethoven's 5th Symphony with its four fanfare-like notes. Apart from the already known technical innovations of the Zeitwerk watch family, this watch's striking mechanism announces each of the quarter-hours with a high tone before sounding a lower note at the full hour, resulting in the famous Leitmotiv when time-lapsed. The Lange Zeitwerk Striking Time is the first Lange wristwatch with an acoustic signature.

A particular challenge was the manufacturing of the tone spirals. Their steel is specially hardened, applying an elaborate several-step process. The difficulty consists in providing the desired sound to the tone spirals. For it to work the two hammers, their striking angle and velocity must be matched precisely. Only a few specialists master this art, which is one of the craft's best-kept secrets.

The constant-force escapement of the Zeitwerk models generates much force, which must be partially absorbed by a fan propeller. Within the Kaliber L043.2 of the Lange Zeitwerk Striking Time this surplus energy is provided to the striking mechanism. Two fusee or snail discs turn on an axle around each other once every hour and tension the springs for the two tone hammers. In the case of the hour hammer, the spring falls off after completing the turn and strikes against the tone spiral. The quarter-hour hammer is activated three times per revolution and creates the strikes every fifteen minutes. The patented barrel construction provides the enormous amount of energy required, particularly for the synchronized switching of all three discs at the full hour. The familiar winding and unwinding principle is literally turned on its head because the barrel disc turns inside of the low-friction bearing when unwinding. The bearing of the barrel, with a higher friction, is only used when the watch is wound up. The result is this requires somewhat more effort to wind up the watch, but there is more energy in the winding spring available for powering the watch. Also, the size of the winding spring can be smaller while maintaining its energy output.

The striking mechanism of the watch not only offers something for the ear, as

The Lange Zeitwerk Striking Time. One can observe the hammer performing its duty between five and seven o'clock.

The Lange Zeitwerk Striking Time. One can observe the hammer performing its duty between five and seven o'clock.

through the glass you can see the specially shaped black-polished premium steel tone hammers. During the minute before completion of each quarter-hour and full hour one can observe how the corresponding tone hammer slowly winds up towards the center of the watch to strike its tone spring in synchronization with the switch of the jumping numerals. These lie between the dial and the bezel and are visible. If desired, the striking mechanism can be paused; for example, if you do not want to be disturbed during meetings. The function of the quarter-hour strike—both rare and useful—can be switched off by pressing the button at four o'clock, which deviates the hammers from the tone spirals so that the striking mechanism stays quiet. When pulling the winding crown, the striking mechanism is automatically disengaged so that the time can be set in both directions. After pushing in the crown or after pressing the button at four o'clock once more the striking mechanism is activated again.

# TWO-BARREL WATCH WITH 31-DAY POWER RESERVE:
## *Lange 31*

None runs longer: the new key-operated manual winding watch by A. Lange & Sons features a power reserve of one month, hence the name Lange 31. An additional innovation—a constant-force escapement—provides constant impulse across the entire runtime, and for this purpose Lange once again revives the key-operated winding mechanism. The movement of the waxing and waning moon has fascinated humans since ancient times, so much so that the oldest calendars based their time calculation on the period from new moon to new

Lange 31, reference: 130.032
**Movement:** Lange manufacture caliber L034.1, key winding. Power reserve of 31 days.
**Functions:** hour and minutes display, small seconds with seconds stop, Lange large date display. Power reserve indicator auf/ab (up/down).
**Case diameter:** 45.9 mm, red gold.
**Dial:** solid silver, argenté
**Hands:** red gold.
**Glass and glass base:** sapphire glass.
**Strap:** hand-sewn croco band with red gold clasp.

moon. Building a mechanical wristwatch with a power reserve of a full calendar month that is also accurate across its entire runtime is one of the few records not yet established in watchmaking, but now this challenge has been met with the Lange 31: a programmatic name for a powerhouse with the heretofore unheard-of power reserve of thirty-one days with a constant impulse. The horological year is divided into twelve winding operations. To store this much energy, the Lange 31

Movement of the Lange 31, Lange manufacture caliber L034.1, key winding, power reserve of 31 days. Finely adjusted in five positions. Double barrel, constant-force escapement for controlled torque delivery, patented two-disc mechanism for displaying the large date, seconds stop mechanism. Plates and bridges from natural nickel silver, hand-engraved balance cock. Diameter: 37.3 mm. Height: 9.6 mm.

features two barrels—one over the other—with a 25-mm interior diameter. Three-quarters of the movement's area is occupied by the portly double barrel. At 1,850 mm each, the two winding springs are five to ten times longer than those in conventional mechanical wristwatches. Winding up such sturdy springs with the delicate mechanics of the crown winding mechanism would be rather cumbersome, so the designers at Lange went back to the "key technology" of earlier pocket watches. The lever effect of the key allows the choice of a smaller transmission than a crown winding mechanism. With a pinion square on the key that is inserted into a notch at the sapphire glass base, the winding energy reaches the barrel. A freewheel integrated

Constant-force escapement of the Lange 31, Lange manufacture caliber L034.1. A mechanism located between the barrel and the escapement of the Lange 31 provides for even torque delivery over the entire runtime and therefore for an accurate rate: a pre-tensioned impulse spiral is re-tensioned sixty degrees every ten seconds. During the following ten seconds the always constant amount of energy is delivered to the escapement.

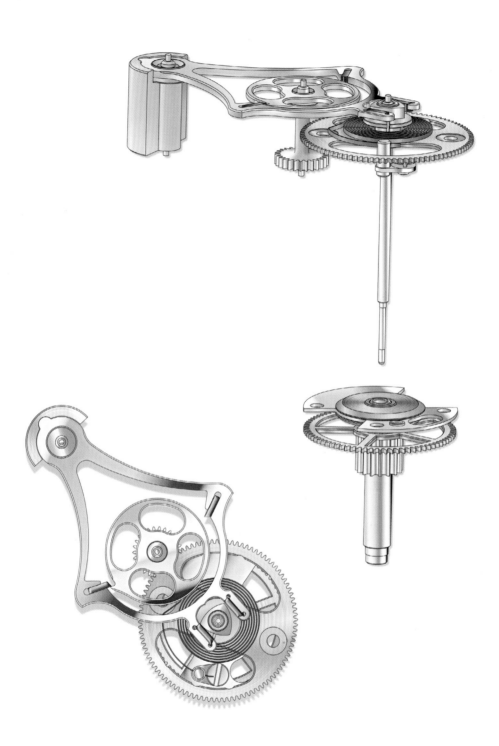

Winding key of the Lange 31, Lange manufacture caliber L034.1. It was custom-designed and adjusted for this watch. It allows for a significantly higher winding ratio with respect to a winding crown. This requires less winding turns—the energy is created faster and more comfortably. It features a mechanism to limit the torque, preventing accidental over-winding of the springs.

Winding spring of the Lange 31. The double barrel houses two winding springs with a length of 1,850 mm. When fully wound they store an energy of over three joules.

into the crown key allows for smooth winding operation just as with a conventional crown, and a torque limiter prevents accidental overwinding of the springs. Certainly a watch movement with such a high power reserve could run over such a long time with a stable rate without further technical provisions. The laws of physics define that an unwinding spring continuously loses its initial torque. With diminishing torque, the amplitude of the balance decreases and accuracy suffers. To overcome this ironclad law, Leonardo da Vinci invented the string and snail mechanism. It takes advantage of the leverage that mostly compensates for the diminishing torque of the spring. This principle of fusee-chain transmission is utilized in two Lange watches of the modern era: the Tourbillon "Pour le Mérite" and the Tourbograph "Pour le Mérite." But with a thirty-one day power reserve, this construction would have been impossible due to the dimensions of the required parts. So Lange searched for another solution and he found it. It consists of a constant-force escapement between the double barrel and escapement. This elaborate construction always provides—that is, independent of the winding state of the spring—constant energy to the escapement section. The mechanism causes a pre-tensioned impulse spiral on the seconds wheel axle to always transmit an even amount of energy to the escapement wheel. Every ten seconds this spiral, affixed to a stud, is tensioned at its outer edge another sixty degrees.

There is still the need to precisely and reliably control this process. This task is fulfilled by the balance. Not only does it provide for the even run of the seconds axle that displays the exact time, but at the same time it also causes the cyclic winding of the constant-force escapement.

Lange 31, reference: 130.025 F
**Movement:** Lange manufacture caliber L034.1, key winding. Power reserve of 31 days.
**Functions:** hour and minutes display, small seconds with seconds stop, Lange large date display. Power reserve indicator auf/ab (up/down).
**Case diameter:** 45.9 mm, platinum.
**Dial:** solid silver, rhodié.
**Hands:** rhodium-plated gold.
**Glass and glass base:** sapphire glass.
**Strap:** hand-sewn croco band with platinum clasp.

This is done via a Reuleaux triangle, a cam disc shaped like an equilateral triangle with convex sides that is affixed to the seconds wheel axle. Every ten seconds—that is, after every sixty degree turn—it activates a cleverly constructed swiveling lever. At its inside, two palettes alternately reach into a wheel with only one tooth that is connected with the barrel via gears and arrest its run every 180-degree turn. With each turn the described impulse spiral is quickly re-tensioned a little and the absorbed energy is passed on to the anchor wheel for the next ten seconds. Although the torque curve within these ten seconds varies slightly, the average energy transmission remains constant for thirty-one days.

The movement of the constant-force escapement—which from the outside looks like an escapement—can be viewed through the sapphire glass base. A transparent sapphire jewel allows viewing of the captivating play between the triangular cam disc and swiveling lever. The constant-force escapement prevents the decreasing torque from the double barrel to negatively influence the rate of the watch. The result: even energy transmission, same amplitude, and same rate accuracy until the thirty-first day, then a cutoff mechanism stops the watch movement. Theoretically, it could continue to run, but this would mean the power of the pulling spring would fall below the

torque of the additional spiral and the escapement would not function properly.

The method of the constant impulse preoccupied even Ferdinand Adolph Lange. He invented a constant force escapement around 1866 for his precision pocket watches with a jumping seconds, a so-called "seconds remontoir." A similar construction was later developed for the large clock at the Lange headquarters, with its almost thirty-three-foot-long pendulum, which still displays the correct time to the employees in Glashütte. Some 140 years later, his watchmaking descendants have continued on this successful path with the newly developed Kaliber L034.1 and the thirty-one-day power reserve. The result is an outstanding timepiece for daily use whose practical applications are obvious. It shows the precise time longer than any other mechanical winding watch, even if you do not wear it for a few days or even weeks. The watch follows the Lange tradition of useful innovation. The platinum case of the Lange 31 has an impressive 46 mm diameter and a height of 15.9 mm. This much stored time needs space, and space is also required by the thirty-one-day power reserve, which takes up almost half the right side of the solid silver dial. It is the succinct and distinctive mark of an innovative watchmaking specialty. Its last segment in red reminds the wearer after a full month it is time again to wind up the watch. The Lange large date on the left side provides a harmonious counterweight. And of course the Lange 31 houses all of the visible quality features under its sapphire glass base that have made A. Lange & Sons watches so sought-after worldwide: screwed balance, whiplash precision index adjuster on the hand-engraved balance cock, screwed gold chatons, and a consummate decoration in the classic Lange style.

# THE GRANDE COMPLICATION - A RESURRECTION

Portraits of the Renaissance often feature sovereigns or noblemen with their watches—a sign that they were objects with a high value and price. There is proof in the form of bills in the archives of cities and nobility. They show that watchmakers in the sixteenth century commanded 500 guilders for such a rare piece, and Albrecht Dürer bought his five-story home in Nuremberg for 275 guilders.

Today, where time is a basic and cheap commodity, this is only understandable when you look at a family of watches that is still entirely exclusive: the Grande Complication. These watches go for between 200,000 and over a million Euros ($219,000 to $1,097,775). Usually they feature everything the art of watchmaking can offer: perpetual calendar, tourbillon, chronograph rattrapante, and a moon phase display. Such representational watches were and are still very much in demand and sought.

In 2001, the head of the Lange atelier for historic Lange pocket watches received an old pocket watch from a visitor to the plant to have it checked. The fact that this watch had to be something special was immediately obvious. It was extraordinarily large and heavy and featured a wonderful engraved case in the style of professor Graff. Unfortunately, the interior of the watch was a total disaster. All of the parts were dirty, and many of them were oxidized so that their original shape could only be guessed. Only the enamel dial consisting of eight parts was unusually well preserved in almost-new condition.

The serial number on a bridge said 42.500. According to the books it belonged to a one-of-a-kind gem with probably the most complicated, most rare, and historically important movement that had ever left the manufacture of A. Lange & Sons, one which was never built again. The pocket watch with the number 42.500 was sold to a Viennese individual in 1902 for 5,600 marks; equivalent to the price of a small house. This watch features a wealth of fascinating complications: apart from the self-striking mechanism with large and small chimes, there is a minutes repetition, a split-seconds hand chronograph with minutes counter and jumping seconds, a perpetual calendar, and a moon phase display. Its nickel-plated nickel-silver movement in the 1A-version consists of an astounding 833 parts. The total weight with case is almost 300 grams (10 ounces). It is a watch of incalculable historical value.

This one-off watch sold in 1902 is perhaps the most complicated pocket watch by A. Lange & Sons. The outstanding features of this nickel silver movement in 1A quality are: a self-striking mechanism with large and small chimes, a minutes repetition, a split-seconds chronograph with minutes counter and jumping seconds, and a perpetual calendar with moon phase display.

But the deplorable condition of the watch raised the question of how to treat such a rare and complex watch. Should one conserve the watch and put it on display?

This solution was never seriously considered. Rather, the decision was made to investigate the function and finish of the individual parts based on the existing substance, to document it, and to completely restore the functionality of the individual mechanisms. This was a chance to conserve the masterful artistry of past watchmakers of past times. What good is a handful of rust which, although authentic, does not allow anyone to know how it once looked and how it worked? So the goal was to conserve as many of the original parts as possible and to restore the venerable movement's beauty. This more than anything meant a lot of research, because this watch had many secrets that were hard to uncover. There were parts whose function was not even clear to an expert. There were other parts that had to be replaced and whose shapes were impossible to reconstruct. Every layer revealed brought new questions. For example, how to fabricate the special kind of tone spring when there were no instructions to be found whatsoever. Sometimes it took months to find a satisfying solution. Sometimes the first effort was successful. And some secrets are still not yet revealed. In the end, it took until 2009 for the pocket watch with the number 42.500 to shine with its vintage gleam.

Perhaps this particular watch will inspire the young watchmakers at Lange to create something similar in a wristwatch format, or to at least revive one or the other complications anew. Watches with chimes or jumping seconds are still missing in today's program, but one can be certain that will change in the next few years.

# Experienced Passion:
# A Visit to the Plant

If you are a fan and enthusiast of A. Lange & Söhne watches, or if you want to become one, you should seriously consider a visit to the plant in Glashütte. This is the only way to grasp the kind of attention to detail and the meticulousness that is applied to making watches. These transindustrial manufacturing methods are more reminiscent of artisan craftwork than they are of factory-made watchmaking. Today, some 500 employees work at the Lange plant. About half of them are watchmakers; that is, they are directly involved in the creation of fine Lange watches. But there are also designers, toolmakers, and operators of CNC machines that are part of the active manufacturing process. They make up another large portion of the staff. If you have had the chance to look over a master watchmaker's shoulder at the Lange plant while they are performing their highly complicated work you will understand how much craftwork, precision, and especially passion is put into the timepieces signed "A. Lange & Söhne." This requires a little round trip, as the staff at Lange now occupies three buildings.

The 16,000 square foot Lange 1 building was inaugurated on December 23, 1993, after full restoration, and houses assembly, in-house tool manufacturing, the atelier of the prototype builders, and the purchasing department. The building dates from the 1920s and used to be owned by Strasser & Rohde, which used to make precision pendulum clocks there.

Since October 22, 2003, Lange I features a glass annex with the new integrated technology and development center. This is where the ideas for future Lange watches come from. The modern glass and steel construction of the new technology and development center is the fifth building, but it is the first new construction of the company that was re-founded in 1990.

Showroom of the manufacturing plant in Glashütte.

172

Engraving burins of different widths, tools for
engravers, and a burin holder.

Architecturally, it not only builds a
symbolic bridge between tradition and
modernity: in the future, watchmakers at
Lange 1 will reach the new wing via a
glass passage. This makes the proverbial
short distances at Lange become reality,
as a large part of the development divi-
sions, such as watch movement construction, prototype production, and technology
are located on a single level. Eighty jobs
in 16,000 square feet will contribute to the
continuing qualitative development of the

company, particularly in the creative and
innovative watchmaking division. The
thirty-two contractor companies needed
only thirteen months to build Lange 1, from
excavating the up to twenty-six foot deep
building pit to the shell construction and
the design of the facades, with over 8,100
square feet of glass panels and including
fourteen miles of data cables, and the
greenery on the roof. About 10 million
Euros ($11,000,500) were invested in eco-
nomic times complicated even for the

luxury segment. After a planning period of ten years a dream of Lange founder Walter Lange—today the representative of the company—and the late Günter Blümlein (who died in 2001) became a reality. As early as 1993—a year before the world premier of the new watch collection of A. Lange & Sons—the two visionaries had the first ideas for a proprietary manufacture of balance springs, the heart of every mechanical watch. With the increase in vertical range manufacture, several Lange specialists have intensely studied the theoretical bases and the fifty-six technological processes applied to making springs. From the pulling of the wire down to a gauge of 0.05 millimeters to the rolling, coiling, and glowing, to the bending—all of the steps involved in making springs for the various Lange watch movements can now be manufactured in-house at the highest quality. However, only a part of

A case base is engraved based on a drawing.

During the finissage every part of a Lange movement receives an elaborate surface treatment. Here a tourbillon cage is polished.

the needs of Lange are covered by in-house manufacturing, so the close relationship with Swiss spring manufacturer Nivarox will continue to exist, as they offer competitive prices and good service.

With the proprietary spring manufacture at Lange a historical circle is closed, as Richard Lange—son of company founder Ferdinand Adolph Lange—applied for a patent as early as 1930 for a "metal alloy for watch springs" (patent no. 529945 from February 19, 1930). Even though Richard Lange would not realize the technical application of his patent since he died two years after the patent was granted, he had laid the decisive foundation for the material composition that is still utilized. Hence, Reinhard Meis rightfully states in his book *A. Lange & Söhne - Eine Uhrmacher-Dynastie aus Dresden* (*A. Lange & Sons - A watchmaker*

*dynasty from Dresden*): " … undisputable is the fact that in every Swiss watch with a Nivarox spring, as it is still to be found today in all quality mechanical watches, a little bit of Lange vibrates along with it."

Saxon ingenuity has not only characterized the development of Lange in the past. Watchmaking innovations, ambitious new movement designs, and a continually increasing depth of production were and still remain paramount for the future growth of the company.

The technology and design center harmoniously fits into the existing ensemble of buildings, which includes Lange II, as well as the Lange watchmaking school, inaugurated in 1998. The newly opened historic Lange headquarters (2001) is located within eyesight at Ferdinand-Adolph-Lange square.

The production facility called Lange II was created in 1922, in the manufacturing plant of the former Archimedes calculating machine factory, and in 1997 was opened as the second Lange building after being thoroughly renovated. In 27,000 square feet one finds the manufacturing section and large parts of the administration. There is also the showroom that fills the second floor of the building. A third building, the Lange headquarters, was inaugurated on December 7, 2001. This former residential and manufacturing building built by Adolph Lange in 1873 is also the building where Walter

Relief engraving of a solid gold base for a watch by A. Lange & Söhne.

Lange—great-grandson of the founder—spent his early years. In April 2000, the building was repurchased from the municipality and later refurbished into a spacious production facility with 1,600 square feet of effective area. Today it houses the watchmaker school, the finishing and engraving departments, service, and part of administration.

When strolling around the company buildings one can observe techniques such as perlage, polishing, engraving, and assembling, depending on the workstation. If you own a Lange watch you might be lucky to shake the hand of the employee who engraved the balance cock of your watch.

Since its comeback Lange has developed over thirty entirely new mechanical watch movements; several thousand parts that are all assembled, adjusted, and decorated in different ways. The resulting variety of work processes makes it unavoidable to apply division of labor and specialization. Next to the assembling and decorating departments there is a studio where only Lange chronographs are adjusted. Despite this partial specialization, the work for the Lange master watchmakers is always challenging and varied. As it is quite difficult to find good watchmakers on a global level, Lange Uhren GmbH in part trains its own up-and-coming professionals in-house. Since 1997, Lange has provided its own watchmaker apprenticeship. It takes about three years to complete.

# Anniversary Models, Special Editions, and, Unfortunately, Some Fakes

Collectors are special people. They usually want what is available only to a precious few to prove their connoisseurship. Watchmakers accommodate this fact by releasing special editions or anniversary models. A. Lange & Sons has brought to market several noteworthy anniversary models and special editions, such as the Tourbillon "Pour le Mérite" (platinum 50/ gold 150), the Lange 1a (100 yellow gold), the Lange Tourbillon (platinum 150/red gold 250), the anniversary Langematik with enamel dial (platinum 500), and the Grosse Lange 1 Luna Mundi, which was only available as a double pack consisting of red and white gold in 101 sets.

The limited edition of the 1815 Mondphase (150 platinum/250 red gold) with a black dial from 1999 is one of the most highly sought after collector items from Lange. They are characterized by an artistic depiction of the Big Dipper, perhaps the most well-known constellation. Watches of this rarity in good condition may command three times the price they originally cost at watch auctions.

The anniversary collection "165 Years - Homage to F. A. Lange" is a reminiscence of the founder of fine German watchmaking and to the groundbreaking creations of the manufacture he built, one that has made possible a mythos that now spans four generations. With three impressive timepieces providing a new technological and aesthetic expression to the Saxon watchmaking dynasty, the Lange watchmakers of the twenty-first century honor the heritage of their great ancestor.

All three new models feature a new and exclusively developed case material. With a Vickes hardness of over 300, the honey-colored, custom-made 18-carat gold is about twice as hard as other gold alloys. Under the hand-engraved balance cock from the same material breathes an in-house developed balance spring as the symbol of the innovative powers residing in each timepiece from Lange. A guilloche

The dial of the 1815 Mondphase (moon phase) is additionally adorned with the zodiac of the Big Dipper. Only 400 watches were built in 1999 and were quickly sold out, as were most limited editions. With a 35.9 mm diameter, this manual winding watch is rather diminutive by today's standards.

dial from solid gold and a ray ribbing on the three-quarter plate of the 1815 Mondphase inspired by historic models, as well as the crown wheel cock of the Lange 1 Tourbillon, indicate the impressive craftsmanship tradition of the brand. If you look at the three watches and the ideas that were realized with them, they do add weight to the Lange motto "Tradition, state-of-the-art." It is as alive in Lange pocket watches from former times as it is with the works of today's watchmakers. The superlative of excellence is the Tourbograph; in 2005, A. Lange & Sons presented the Tourbograph "Pour le Mérite," a large complication that set new standards for fine watchmaking—the first minute tourbillon in a wristwatch format with impulse via fusee and chain and an additional rattrapante chronograph. The complexity of the movement allows for only one watch to be made per month. The presentation of the second partial collection of fifty units in a gold alloy "yet to be determined" was announced way back. The tourbograph "Pour le Mérite," which honors Ferdinand Adolph Lange, was now presented in a new and harder gold and not only embodies Lange's claim to build the best watches in the world, but is also proof that even a watchmaking superlative can be improved. For the new millennium, A. Lange & Sons presented the Lange 1 Tourbillon based on the legendary Lange 1. Back then it was still impossible what the Lange designers managed to achieve a few years later: to stop the balance inside the rotating tourbillon cage directly and without delay. With this they added the missing piece to the tourbillon which was considered the watchmaking paragon for over 200 years. The artistic movement which achieves optimal rate accuracy by defeating gravity could not be stopped, hence it could not be set precisely down to the second. The solution to this problem—a patented seconds stop mechanism —is now also found inside the Lange 1 Tourbillon of the anniversary collection. It can be observed through the transparent ring of the large date with sapphire glass and it stands for the Lange maxim to even doubt perfection itself. The crowning feature of this rarity is a highly polished and precisely inserted cock of honey-colored gold that supports the tourbillon pivoting cage on the dial side. Further special characteristics include that the minutes tourbillon is supported by a diamond endstone, a hallmark of excellence that Adolph Lange started to incorporate to label the 1A top quality of his pocket watches.

For the new 1815 Mondphase, an extraordinarily precise moon phase gear was designed. Due to a gear train with a special transmission there is only a 6.61-second deviation per moon phase, which leads to a deviation of only a single day from the actual moon's orbit over the course of 1,058 years. If such a watch had existed in 952—around the time of German Kaiser Otto the Great—and had it run without stopping until today, then its moon phase of 2010 would have had to be corrected for the first time. The watch was limited to 265 units.

A rather not so nice subject, but one that must be mentioned, is the question of authenticity. There are very few if any problems concerning fake watches in the case of Lange. Whatever they are offering on the internet as a "Grosse Lange 1," "Tourbobraph 'Pour le Mérite,'" or as a "Flyback Tourbillon" for 199 Euros ($219) is no more than a bad caricature of a genuine Lange watch. Anyone who has read this book and studied the images of the Lange movements will not be fooled by these concoctions. An expert recognizes such fakes from a distance of ten feet and will most likely not hesitate to tell you about it.

While brands like Rolex or IWC have trouble spotting good fakes, the sapphire glass base of every Lange watch ensures that the wheat is separated from the chaff right away. No counterfeiter can afford to finish a movement in such a manner. Although by now there are Chinese movements, such as the caliber 944, which is well-finished by machine and made by old

tool machines for the Venus caliber 175, but it is still miles away from a Lange watch as to finish. No other watch has a greater imbalance between the original and the fake. For this reason it is not appropriate to present images of fake Lange watches. It would be a sacrilege. Should you ever see such a watch, you will immediately understand my point. An additional protection against fakes is the "book for the watch," which will now accompany every Lange watch. As the world's first manufacturer, Lange presents a unique document that will accompany every valuable Lange watch across several generations of owners. Repairs and revisions are documented in handwriting by the Lange service watchmakers. The personal family register of every Lange watch opens a new chapter regarding service quality and custome service. The precious timepieces of A. Lange & Sons are the result of a time-consuming and elaborate process. The Saxon master watchmakers require several months to assemble and finish each watch by hand. They create masterpieces for a small eternity that provide joy to their owners over generations —masterpieces with supreme heritage.

With the "book for the watch" Lange has created a medium that documents the lifetime of a Lange watch from the very first moment of its use and describes the relevant service and details by A.

Lange & Sons. Since July 1, 2004, all watches are delivered with this exclusive little book. The Saxons are once again one step ahead of everyone else: they were the first watch brand to offer this service book to their customers.

Inside the "book for the watch," the owners of a Lange will find the following elements: the seal of quality of Lange on the first page, serving as proof for warranty claims and replacing the former warranty card in a credit card format. The section "A masterpiece for generations" is where the owner of the watch can register. If one wants to gift or pass on the watch, one has the option to add a dedication. This way, the path of the watch can be traced over generations. The foundation for Lange service shows how important it is to have a revision performed on a regular basis. The owner of a Lange watch can honor his appreciation by bringing it in for service regularly, assuring the long-term value of the watch.

Based on the service registry at the end of the book all of the service checks can be traced. The performed operations are detailed by the service provider himself. Every watch receives its fully replicable "vita." Only Lange service centers are authorized to fill out service cards and to affix the Lange seal of quality to them. The service of a Lange watch is so demanding that it is reserved for specially trained master watchmakers. This assures that the Lange watch will show the time in 100 years as precisely as the watches made at Lange for the past 100 years. The value of a used watch always depends on the quality of the documentation. For models before 2004, this includes the warranty card, packaging, and other accessories.

With the Datograph Auf/Ab (up/down) with classic column wheel switch, precisely jumping minutes counter and flyback function are now offered in a chronograph with only a 41 mm diameter that also features a power reserve indicator at six o'clock. Enlarging the large date some four percent preserved the harmonious proportions of the dial design.

# Appendix

## Timetable of the History of A. Lange & Söhne

**1815** Ferdinand Adolph Lange is born February 18.

**1830** Lange begins his apprenticeship with future court watchmaker Gutkaes.

**1837** Lange's journeyman years lead him to Paris, England, and Switzerland. He begins writing his famous sketchbook.

**1841** Gutkaes builds the famous "digital" five-minute watch for the newly built Desden Semper Opera.

**1842** Lange receives his master title, becomes partner of the company of his teacher, and marries his daughter Antonia.

**1843** Lange suggests to the Saxon government to industrially produce watches in the impoverished Erzgebirge region.

**1845** By creating the Glashütte Manufaktur "Lange & Cie." on December 7, Lange lays the foundation for fine watchmaking in Saxony. A few days later his first son Richard is born.

**1846** With the introduction of the metric system into watchmaking Lange improves the precise calculation and manufacturing of parts.

**1848** As its mayor, Lange engages politically for the city of Glashütte during the next eighteen years.

**1864** To improve movement stability Lange introduces the three-quarter plate.

**1867** Lange becomes an illustrious citizen of Glashütte.

**1868** Richard Lange becomes partner of his father's company, from now on called "A. Lange & Söhne." His younger brother Emil follows him a few years later.

**1873** Lange headquarters is built. It is both home and workshop and houses a precision clock with a nine-meter (29.5-foot) long pendulum.

**1875** Ferdinand Adolph Lange dies December 3. His sons continue to manage the company.

**1895** Glashütte erects a monument for the fifteith anniversary of the company.

controls: crown for winding the watch and adjusting time

case dimensions: diameter 40.5 mm; height 10.7 mm, limited edition of 50 units in platinum and 200 units in red gold

movement dimensions: diameter 31.6 mm; height 6.0 mm; glass and base:

sapphire glass (hardness 9)

dial: three-part enamel dial

hands: blued steel

watch strap: hand-sewn croco band with solid Lange pin buckle in platinum or red gold

---

# 2. DATA SHEET TOURBOGRAPH "POUR LE MÉRITE"

watch movement: Lange manufacture caliber L903.0, manual winding, created following the highest Lange quality criteria and assembled and decorated by hand; finely adjusted in five positions; plates and bridges from natural nickel silver; hand-engraved chronograph bridge; 30.0 mm diameter; height 8.9 mm

parts watch movement: 465 (without chain), and of these: pivoting cage: 84; parts chain: over 600

bearing jewels: 43, 2 diamond endstones; screwed gold chatons: 6

oscillation system: shock-proof glucydur spring balance, Nivarox 1 spiral with an oscillating frequency of 21,600 half-oscillations per hour (3 Herz)

power reserve: 36 hours after fully wound

functions: hour, minutes, power reserve, minutes tourbillon with fusee and chain, chronograph with rattrapante function

controls: crown for winding the watch and adjusting the time, chrono button at two o'clock, zero reset at four o'clock, rattrapante button at ten o'clock

case dimensions: diameter 41.2 mm; height 14.3 mm; platinum; glass and base: anti-glare sapphire glass (hardness 9)

dial: solid silver, argenté

hands: blued steel, chrono hands from gilded steel

watch strap: hand-sewn croco band with solid Lange pin buckle in platinum

limited edition: total of 101 units: 51 in platinum and 50 in gold at a later date

# 3. DATA SHEET CABARET TOURBILLON

**watch movement:** Lange manufacture caliber L042.1, manual winding, created following the highest Lange quality criteria and assembled and decorated by hand; finely adjusted in five positions; three-quarter plate from natural nickel silver; Lange large date; hand-engraved idle wheel and tourbillon cock

**watch parts:** 373, 84 of which are inside the pivot cage

**bearing jewels:** 47, 2 diamond endstones; screwed gold chatons: 9

**escapement:** anchor escapement

**oscillation system:** shock-proof glucydur spring manufactured in-house, oscillating frequency of 21,600 half-oscillations per hour, whiplash precision index adjuster and patented drop-off regulation

**power reserve:** 5 days after fully wound

**functions:** time display with hour, minutes, small seconds; power reserve indicator; minutes tourbillon with patented seconds stop

**controls:** crown for winding the watch and adjusting the time, date correction push button at two o'clock (recessed)

**case dimensions:** 39.2 x 29.5 mm; height 10.3 mm; platinum or red gold

**case dimensions:** 22.3 x 32.6 x 6.35 mm; glass and glass base: sapphire glass (hardness 9)

**dial:** solid silver, rhodié, or argenté

**hands:** rhodium-plated gold with solid Lange folding clasp

**watch strap:** finest croco band with solid Lange folding clasp in solid platinum or red gold

# 4. DATA SHEET LANGEMATIK PERPETUAL IN RED GOLD

**watch movement:** L922.1 Sax-0-Mat, automatic winding, created following the highest Lange quality criteria and assembled and decorated by hand; finely adjusted in five positions; three-quarter plate from natural cross-rolled nickel silver with integrated three-quarter rotor from 21-carat gold and platinum segment, reversing and reduction gear with four ball bearings; hand-engraved balance cock

**parts watch movement:** 478

**bearing jewels:** 43

**escapement:** anchor escapement

**oscillation system:** shock-proof glucydur screw balance, Nivarox spiral, oscillating frequency of 21,600 half-oscillations per hour, whiplash precision index adjuster

**power reserve:** 46 hours after fully wound

**functions:** hour display, seconds stop with

zero reset mechanism, perpetual calendar with large date, moon phase display, day, month, four-year and leap year indicator, day and night indicator

**controls:** crown for winding up and adjusting time, main button for simultaneous adjustment of all calendar functions as well as one day, one month, and one moon correction button (recessed)

**case:** diameter 38.5 mm, red gold; glass and glass base: sapphire glass (hardness 9)

**dial:** solid silver, argenté

**hands:** red gold, noctilucent

**clasp:** croco band with solid Lange pin buckle in red gold

## 5. DATA SHEET DATOGRAPH PERPETUAL

**watch movement:** Lange manufacture caliber L952.1, manual winding, created following the highest Lange quality criteria and assembled and decorated by hand; finely adjusted in five positions; plates and bridges of natural nickel silver, hand-engraved balance cock

**parts watch movement:** 556

**bearing jewels:** 45; screwed gold chatons: 4

**escapement:** anchor escapement

**oscillation system:** shock-proof glucydur balance with eccentric adjustment; balance spring of the highest quality with patented mounting (spiral clamp), oscillating frequency of 18,000 half-oscillations per hour, fine adjustment of drop-off with lateral adjustment screw and whiplash spring

**power reserve:** 36 hours after fully wound

**functions:** flyback chronograph with precisely jumping minutes counter; perpetual calendar with large date, moon phase, day, month, four-year and leap year indicators, day and night indicator, hour, minutes, small seconds with seconds stop, and tachymeter scale

**controls:** crown to wind up and adjust the time, two buttons for controlling the chronograph, main button for simultaneous adjustment of all calendar functions as well as one day, one month, and one moon correction button (recessed)

**case dimensions:** diameter 41 mm, platinum

**glass and glass base:** anti-glare sapphire glass (hardness 9)

**dial:** solid silver, rhodié

**hands:** rhodinized gold; seconds chrono hands from blued steel

**watch strap:** hand-sewn croco band with solid Lange pin buckle in platinum

# 6. DATA SHEET LANGE DOUBLE SPLIT

**watch movement:** Lange manufacture caliber L001.1, manual winding, created following the highest Lange quality criteria and assembled and decorated by hand; finely adjusted in five positions; plates and bridges from natural cross-rolled nickel silver; hand-engraved balance cock

**parts watch movement:** 465

**bearing jewels:** 40, screwed gold chatons: 4

**escapement:** anchor escapement

**oscillation system:** new shock-proof glucydur balance with eccentric adjustments, balance spring of the highest quality made in-house with patented mounting (spiral clamp); oscillating frequency of 21,600 half-oscillations per hour, drop-off adjustment with whiplash spring

**power reserve:** 38 hours after fully wound

**functions:** world's first flyback chronograph with double rattrapante controlled via classic column wheels, precisely jumping chrono minutes counter and rattrapante minutes counter, flyback functions, isolator mechanism, hour, minutes, small seconds with seconds stop, power reserve, additional and split time measurement between 1/6 of a second and 30 minutes, and tachymeter

**controls:** crown for winding up and adjusting the watch, two buttons for controlling the chronograph, one button to control the rattrapante

**case dimensions:** diameter 43 mm, platinum; glass and glass bottom: sapphire glass (hardness 9)

**dials:** solid silver, two-part, black

**hands:** yellow gold, rhodium-plated gold, blued and rhodium-plated steel

**watch strap:** hand-sewn croco band with solid Lange pin buckle in platinum

# 7. DATA SHEET 1815 CHRONOGRAPH

**watch movement:** Lange manufacture caliber L951.5, manual winding, created following the highest Lange quality criteria and assembled and decorated by hand; finely adjusted in five positions; plates and bridges from natural nickel silver; hand-engraved balance cock

**parts watch movement:** 306

**bearing jewels:** 40; screwed gold chatons: 4 **escapement:** anchor escapement

**oscillation system:** shock-proof glucydur balance with eccentric adjustment; balance cock of the highest quality manufactured in-house, oscillating frequency of 18,000 half-oscillations per hour, fine adjustment of drop-off with lateral adjustment screw and whiplash spring

**power reserve:** 60 hours after fully wound: flyback chronograph with precisely jumping minutes counter; time display with hour, minutes, small seconds with seconds stop

**controls:** crown for winding and adjusting time, two buttons for controlling the chronograph

**case dimensions:** diameter 39.5 mm; height 10.8 mm

**movement dimensions:** diameter 30.6 mm; height 6.1 mm

**glass and glass base:** sapphire glass (hardness 9)

**references:** 402.032; 402.026

**case:** red gold, white gold

**dial:** depending on the version, silver, argenté

**hands:** blued steel

**watch strap:** depending on the version, hand-sewn croco band red-brown or hand-sewn black croco band

**wrist band:** Lange pin buckle in red gold or Lange pin buckle in white gold

## 8. DATA SHEET DATOGRAPH

**watch movement:** Lange manufacture caliber L951.1, manual winding, created following the highest Lange quality criteria and assembled and decorated by hand; finely adjusted in five positions; plates and bridges from natural nickel silver; hand-engraved balance cock

**parts watch movement:** 405

**bearing jewels:** 40; screwed gold chatons: 4

**escapement:** anchor escapement

**oscillation system:** shock-proof glucydur screw balance, Nivarox 1-spiral with an oscillating frequency of 18,000 half-oscillations per hour, whiplash precision index adjuster and patented drop-off adjustment

**power reserve:** 36 hours after fully wound

**functions:** chronograph with 30-minute counter, flyback and precisely jumping seconds counter; hour, minutes, small seconds with seconds stop, large date

**controls:** crown for winding and adjusting time, two buttons to control the chronograph, one button for quick-adjustment of the large date

**case dimensions:** diameter 39 mm, red gold, platinum, yellow gold

**glass and glass base:** anti-glare sapphire glass (hardness 9)

**dial:** solid silver, argenté

**hands:** red gold or white gold, gilded and blued steel

**watch strap:** hand-sewn croco band with solid Lange pin buckle in red gold, platinum, yellow gold

## 9. DATA SHEET LANGE 1 ZEITZONE

**watch movement:** Lange manufacture caliber L031.1, manual winding, created following the highest Lange quality criteria and assembled and decorated by hand; finely adjusted in five positions; double barrel; plates and bridges from natural nickel silver; hand-engraved balance cock and intermediate-wheel cock

**parts watch movement:** 417

**bearing jewels:** 54; screwed gold chatons: 4

**escapement:** anchor escapement

**oscillation system:** shock-proof glucydur screw balance, Nivarox spiral with an oscillating frequency of 21,600 half-oscillations per hour, whiplash precision index adjuster and patented drop-off adjustment

**power reserve:** over 72 hours after fully wound

**functions:** home time with day/night indicator (hour, minutes, small seconds with seconds stop), zone time (hour, minutes) with day/night indicator and city ring, large date for home time, power reserve indicator

**controls:** crown for winding and adjusting the time; one button for adjusting the large date; one button to adjust the city ring, synchronized with the hour dial of the zone time display and the day/night indicator for the zone time

**case dimensions:** diameter 41.9 mm, 18-carat yellow or red gold or platinum;

**glass and glass base:** anti-glare sapphire glass (hardness 9)

**dial:** solid silver, champagne-color, argenté, rhodié: gold appliqués

**hands:** yellow and red gold or rhodium-plated gold, blued steel

**watch straps:** hand-sewn croco bands with solid Lange pin buckle in gold or platinum

## 10. DATA SHEET CABARET MONDPHASE

**watch movement:** Lange manufacture caliber L931.5, manual winding, created following the highest Lange quality criteria and assembled and decorated by hand; finely adjusted in five positions; plates and bridges from natural cross-rolled nickel silver; hand-engraved balance cock

**parts watch movement:** 268

**bearing jewels:** 31; screwed gold chatons: 3

**escapement:** anchor **escapement:** shock-proof glucydur screw balance, Nivarox 1 spiral with an oscillating frequency of 21,600 half-oscillations per hour, whiplash precision index adjuster and patented drop-off adjustment

**power reserve:** 42 hours after fully wound

**functions:** hour, minutes, small seconds with seconds stop, patented large date, moon phase display

**controls:** crown for winding and adjusting time, two buttons recessed into the case to adjust the large date and the moon phase

**case dimensions:** 36.3 × 25.5 mm, height 9.1 mm, yellow or red gold

**glass and glass base:** sapphire glass (hardness 9)

**dials:** solid silver in champagne or argenté; gold appliqués

**hands:** yellow or red gold

**watch strap:** hand-sewn croco band with solid Lange pin buckle in gold

## 11. DATA SHEET SAXONIA JAHRESKALENDER

**watch movement:** Lange manufacture caliber L085.1 Sax-0-Mat, automatic winding, created following the highest Lange quality criteria and assembled and decorated by hand; finely adjusted in five positions; three-quarter plate from natural nickel silver with integrated three-quarter rotor from 21-carat gold and platinum flywheel mass, reversing and reduction gear with four ball bearings; hand-engraved balance cock

**parts watch movement:** 476

**bearing jewels:** 43

**escapement:** anchor escapement

**oscillation system** shock-proof glucydur screw balance, Nivarox spiral, oscillating frequency of 21,600 half-oscillations per hour, whiplash precision index adjuster and patented drop-off adjustment

**power reserve:** 46 hours after fully wound

**functions:** time display with hour and minutes, small seconds with seconds stop and zero reset function, yearly calendar with patented large date, day of the week, month and moon phase display

**controls:** crown for winding and adjusting the time, one recessed corrective button each for adjusting the large date, day of the week, month and moon phase display

**case dimensions:** diameter 30.4 mm; height 5.4 mm

**references:** 330.026, 330.032

**case:** white gold, red gold

**glass and glass base:** sapphire glass (hardness 9)

**dial:** blued steel; rhodium-plated red gold

**watch strap:** hand-sewn croco band with solid Lange pin buckle in white or red gold

## 12. DATA SHEET LANGE ZEITWERK

**watch movement:** Lange manufacture caliber L043.1, manual winding, created following the highest Lange quality criteria and assembled and decorated by hand; finely adjusted in five positions; three-quarter plate from natural nickel silver; hand-engraved balance cock; jumping minutes; constant impulse via constant force escapement

**parts watch movement:** 388

**bearing jewels:** 66; screwed gold chatons: 2

**escapement:** anchor escapement

**oscillation system:** shock-proof glucydur balance with eccentric adjustments; balance spring of the highest quality from in-house production with patented mounting, oscillating frequency of 18,000 half-oscillations per hour, fine adjustment of the drop-off with lateral adjustment screw and whiplash spring

**power reserve:** 36 hours after fully wound

**functions:** time display with hour and jumping minutes, small seconds with seconds stop, power reserve indicator

**controls:** crown for winding up and adjusting the watch

**case dimensions:** diameter 41.9 mm; height 12.6 mm

**movement dimensions:** diameter 33.6 mm; height 9.3 mm

**references:** 140.021, 140.029, 140.032, 140.025

**case:** yellow gold, white gold, red gold, platinum

**glass and glass base:** sapphire glass (hardness 9)

**dial variations:** solid silver champagne, solid silver black, solid silver argenté, solid silver rhodié, time bridge natural nickel silver, rhodium-plated nickel silver

**hands:** rhodium-plated gold

**watch strap:** hand-sewn croco band with solid Lange pin buckle in gold or platinum

## 13. DATA SHEET RICHARD LANGE "REFERENZUHR"

**watch movement:** Lange manufacture caliber L033.1, manual winding, created following the highest Lange quality criteria and assembled and decorated by hand; finely adjusted in five positions; plates and bridges from natural nickel silver; hand-engraved balance cock

**parts watch movement:** 276

**bearing jewels:** 34; screwed gold chatons: 1

**escapement:** anchor escapement

**oscillation system:** shock-proof glycydur balance with eccentric adjustments; balance spring of highest quality manufactured in-house, oscillating frequency of 21,600 half- oscillations per hour, fine adjustment of drop-off with lateral adjustment screw and whiplash spring

**power reserve:** time display with hour, minutes, small seconds with seconds stop and zero reset mechanism, power reserve indicator

**controls:** crown for winding the watch and for adjusting time, button for zero reset of the seconds hand

**case dimensions:** diameter 40.5 mm; height 11.2 mm

**glass and glass base:** sapphire glass (hardness 9)

**watch movement dimensions:** diameter 30.6 mm; height 6.8 mm

**references:** 250.032, 250.025

**case:** red gold and platinum

**dial:** solid silver, argenté; solid silver, rhodié

**limitation:** 75 units/50 units

**hands:** red gold; small seconds: blued steel

**watch strap:** hand-sewn croco band in red-brown, hand-sewn croco band in black

**buckle:** solid Lange pin buckle in red gold, solid Lange pin buckle in platinum.

## 14. DATA SHEET RICHARD LANGE

**watch movement:** Lange manufacture caliber L041.2, manual winding, with central seconds, created following the highest Lange quality criteria and assembled and decorated by hand; finely adjusted in five positions; plates and bridges from natural nickel silver; hand-engraved balance cock

**parts watch movement:** 199

**bearing jewels:** 26; screwed gold chatons: 2

**escapement:** anchor escapement

**oscillation system:** shock-proof glucydur balance with eccentric adjustments; balance spring of highest quality manufactured in-house with patented mounting (spiral clamp), oscillating frequency of 21,600 half-oscillations per hour, fine adjustment of the drop-off with lateral adjustment screw and whiplash spring

**power reserve:** 38 hours after fully wound

**functions:** time display with hour, minutes and seconds

**controls:** crown for winding the watch and adjusting the time with seconds stop

**case dimensions:** diameter 40.5 mm, 18-carat yellow gold, red gold or platinum

**glass and glass base:** anti-glare sapphire glass (hardness 9)

**dial:** solid silver, argenté or rhodié

**hands:** rhodium-plated gold; seconds stop from blued steel

**watch strap:** hand-sewn croco band with solid Lange pin buckle in gold or platinum

## 15. DATA SHEET GROSSE LANGE 1

**watch movement:** Lange manufacture caliber L901.2, manual winding, created following the highest Lange quality criteria and assembled and decorated by hand; finely adjusted in five positions; double barrel; plates and bridges from natural nickel silver; hand-engraved balance cock

**parts watch movement:** 53; screwed gold chatons: 9

**escapement:** anchor escapement

**oscillation system:** shock-proof glucydur screw balance, Nivarox spiral, oscillating frequency of 21,600 half oscillations per hour, whiplash precision index adjuster and patented drop-off adjustment

**power reserve:** over 72 hours when fully wound

**functions:** time display with hour, minutes, small seconds with seconds stop, patented large date, power reserve indicator

**controls:** crown for winding the watch and adjusting time, date correction button

**case dimensions:** diameter 41.9 mm, yellow gold, red gold or platinum

**glass and glass base:** sapphire glass (hardness 9)

**dial:** solid silver, champagne, or rhodié; gold appliqués

**hands:** gold or rhodium-plated gold

**watch strap:** finest croco band with Lange pin buckle in solid gold or platinum

## 16. DATA SHEET SAXONIA

**watch movement:** Lange manufacture caliber L941.1, manual winding, created following the highest Lange quality criteria and assembled and decorated by hand; finely adjusted in five positions; plates and bridges from natural nickel silver; hand-engraved balance cock

**parts watch movement:** 164

**bearing jewels:** 21; screwed gold chatons: 4

**escapement:** anchor escapement

**oscillation system:** shock-proof glucydur screw balance, Nivarox spiral, oscillating frequency of 21,600 half-oscillations per hour, whiplash precision index adjuster and patented drop-off adjustment

**power reserve:** 45 hours after fully wound

**functions:** time display with hour, minutes, small seconds with seconds stop

**controls:** crown for winding the watch and for adjusting time

**case dimensions:** diameter 37.0 mm, yellow, white or red gold

**glass and glass base:** sapphire glass (hardness 9)

**dial:** solid silver, champagne, argenté, black or grey

**hands:** yellow gold, rhodium-plated gold or red gold

**watch strap:** croco band with solid Lange pin buckle in yellow, white or red gold

## 17. DATA SHEET SAXONIA AUTOMATIK AND GROSSE SAXONIA AUTOMATIK

**watch movement:** Lange manufacture caliber L921.4 (Saxonia Automatic) or L921.2 (Large Saxonia Automatic), automatic winding, created following the highest Lange quality criteria and assembled and decorated by hand; finely adjusted in five positions; plates and bridges from natural nickel silver; hand-engraved balance cock

**parts watch movement:** 378 (Saxonia Automatic), 307 (Large Saxonia Automatic)

**bearing jewels:** 45 (Saxonia Automatic), 36 (Large Saxonia Automatic)

**escapement:** anchor escapement

**oscillation system** shock-proof glucydur screw balance, Nivarox spiral, oscillating frequency of 21,600 half-oscillations per hour, whiplash precision index adjuster and patented drop-off adjustment

**power reserve:** 46 hours after fully wound: time display with hour, minutes, small seconds with seconds stop, large date (Saxonia Automatic)

**controls:** crown for winding and adjusting time, button for adjusting the date display (Saxonia Automatic)

**case dimensions:** diameter 37.0 mm (Saxonia Automatic), diameter 40.6 mm (Large Saxonia Automatic), white or red gold

**glass and glass base:** sapphire glass (hardness 9)

**dial:** solid silver, argenté, black or grey

**hands:** rhodium-plated gold or red gold; rhodium-plated seconds hand, red gold or blued steel

**watch strap:** croco band with solid Lange pin buckle in white or red gold

## 18. DATA SHEET 1815

**watch movement:** Lange manufacture caliber L051.1, manual winding, created following the highest Lange quality criteria and assembled and decorated by hand; finely adjusted in five positions; three-quarter plate from natural nickel silver; hand-engraved balance cock

**parts watch movement:** 188

**bearing jewels:** 21; screwed gold chatons: 5

**escapement:** anchor escapement

**oscillation system** shock-proof glucydur screw balance, Nivarox spiral, oscillating frequency of 21,600 half-oscillations per hour, whiplash precision index adjuster and patented drop-off adjustment

**power reserve:** 55 hours after fully wound, minutes, small seconds

**controls:** crown for winding the watch and adjusting time

**case dimensions:** diameter 40.0 mm; height 8.9 mm, yellow gold, white gold, or red gold, or in a limited platinum edition of 500 units

**glass and glass base:** sapphire glass (hardness 9)

**watch movement dimensions:** diameter 30.6 mm, height 4.6 mm

**dial:** solid silver, argenté or rhodié (only platinum)

**hands:** blued steel or rhodium-plated gold (only platinum)

**watch strap:** hand-sewn croco band with solid Lange pin buckle in gold or platinum

## 19. DATA SHEET LANGE 1 DAYMATIC

**watch movement:** Lange manufacture caliber L021.1, automatic winding, created following the highest Lange quality criteria and assembled and decorated by hand; finely adjusted in five positions; central rotor with flywheel mass of platinum; hand-engraved balance cock

**parts watch movement:** 426

**bearing jewels:** 67; screwed gold chatons: 7

**escapement:** anchor escapement

**oscillation system** shock-proof glucydur balance of highest quality manufactured in-house, oscillation frequency of 21,600 half-oscillations per hour, fine adjustment of the drop-off with lateral adjustment screw and whiplash spring

**power reserve:** 50 hours after fully wound

**functions:** time display with hour and minutes, small seconds with seconds stop, patented large date, retrograde day indicator

**controls:** crown for winding the watch and adjusting time, date and day correction buttons

**case dimensions:** diameter 39.5 mm; height 10.4 mm

**glass and glass base:** sapphire glass (hardness 9)

**watch movement dimensions:** diameter 31.6 mm; height: 6.1 mm

**reference:** 320.021, 320.032, 320.025

**case:** yellow gold, red gold, platinum

**dial:** solid champagne silver, solid silver argenté, solid silver rhodié

**hands:** yellow gold, red gold, rhodium-plated gold

**watch strap:** hand-sewn croco band with solid Lange pin buckle in gold or platinum

## 20. DATA SHEET LANGE 1

**watch movement:** Lange manufacture caliber L901.0, manual winding, created following the highest Lange quality criteria and assembled and decorated by hand; finely adjusted in five positions; double barrel; plates and bridges from natural nickel silver; hand-engraved balance cock

**parts watch movement:** 365

**bearing jewels:** 53; screwed gold chatons: 9

**escapement:** anchor escapement

**oscillation system** shock-proof glucydur screw balance, Nivarox spiral, oscillating frequency of 21,600 half-oscillations per hour, whiplash precision index adjuster and patented drop-off adjustment

**power reserve:** over 72 hours after fully wound

**functions:** time display with hour, minutes, small seconds with seconds stop, patented large date, power reserve indicator

**controls:** crown for winding the watch and for adjusting time, date correction button

**case dimensions:** diameter 38.5 mm; height 10 mm; 18-carat white gold

**glass and glass base:** anti-glare sapphire glass (hardness 9)

**watch movement dimensions:** diameter 30.4 mm; height 5.9 mm

**dial:** solid silver argenté; rhodium-plated gold appliqués, noctilucent

**hands:** rhodium-plated gold, noctilucent

**watch strap:** hand-sewn croco band with solid Lange pin buckle in solid white gold

## 21. DATA SHEET GROSSE LANGE 1

**watch movement:** Lange manufacture caliber L901.2, manual winding, created following the highest Lange quality criteria and assembled and decorated by hand; finely adjusted in five positions; double barrel; plates and bridges from natural nickel silver; hand-engraved balance cock

**parts watch movement:** 365

**bearing jewels:** 53; screwed gold chatons: 9

**escapement:** anchor escapement

**oscillation system** shock-proof glucydur screw balance, Nivarox spiral, oscillating frequency of 21,600 half-oscillations per hour, whiplash precision index adjuster and patented drop-off adjustment

**power reserve:** over 72 hours after fully wound

**functions:** time display with hour, minutes, small seconds with seconds stop, patented large date, power reserve indicator

**controls:** crown for winding up the watch and adjusting the time, date correction button

**case dimensions:** diameter 41.9 mm, yellow gold, red gold, or platinum

**glass and glass base:** sapphire glass (hardness 9)

**dial:** solid silver, champagne, argenté or rhodié; gold appliqués

**hands:** gold or rhodium-plated gold

**watch strap:** finest croco band with Lange pin buckle in solid gold or platinum

## 22. DATA SHEET LANGE 31

**watch movement:** Lange manufacture caliber L034.1, manual winding, created following the highest Lange quality criteria and assembled and decorated by hand; finely adjusted in five positions; three-quarter double barrel; plates and bridges from natural nickel silver; hand-engraved balance cock

**parts watch movement:** 406

**bearing jewels:** 61, one transparent sapphire bearing jewel; screwed gold chatons: 3

**escapement:** anchor escapement

**oscillation system** shock-proof glucydur screw balance, Nivarox spiral, oscillating frequency of 21,600 half-oscillations per hour, whiplash precision index adjuster and patented drop-off adjustment

**power reserve:** 31 days after fully wound (744 hours) with shut-off mechanism

**functions:** time display with hour, minutes, small seconds with seconds stop, large date, power reserve display

**controls:** key for winding the watch featuring torque limiter, crown for adjusting time, button for adjusting the date

**case dimensions:** diameter 46 mm, platinum

**glass and glass base:** sapphire glass (hardness 9)

**dial:** rhodium-plated gold

**watch strap:** hand-sewn croco band with solid Lange pin buckle in platinum

---

## 23. DATA SHEET LANGE 1 TOURBILLON

**watch movement:** Lange manufacture caliber L961.2, manual winding, created following the highest Lange quality criteria and assembled and decorated by hand; finely adjusted in five positions; three-quarter plate from natural nickel silver; crown wheel balance with ray ribbing; intermediate wheel and tourbillon cock from honey-colored gold, hand-engraved at the plant

**parts watch movement:** 381

**bearing jewels:** 51; 2 diamond endstones

**escapement:** anchor escapement

**oscillation system** shock-proof glucydur screw balance, balance spring of highest quality manufactured in-house, oscillating frequency of 21,600 half-oscillations per hour, whiplash precison index adjuster

**power reserve:** 72 hours after fully wound

**functions:** time display with hour, minutes, small seconds; Lange large date display; power reserve indicator; minutes tourbillon with patented seconds stop

**controls:** crown for winding the watch and adjusting time, date correction button at ten o'clock

**case dimensions:** diameter 38.5 mm; height: 9.8 mm

**glass and glass base:** anti-glare sapphire glass (hardness 9)

**watch movement dimensions:** diameter 30.6 mm; height 5.9 mm

**case:** honey-colored gold

**watch strap:** hand-sewn, red-brown croco band with solid Lange pin buckle in honey-colored gold

**limitation:** 150 units

## 24. DATA SHEET 1815 MONDPHASE

**watch movement:** Lange manufacture caliber L943.2, manual winding, created following the highest Lange quality criteria and assembled and decorated by hand; finely adjusted in five positions; three-quarter plate from natural nickel silver, with ray ribbing; balance cock from honey-colored gold, hand-engraved

**parts watch movement:** 220

**bearing jewels:** 26

**escapement:** anchor escapement

**oscillation systems:** shock-proof glucydur screw balance, balance spring of the highest quality manufactured in-house, oscillating frequency of 21,600 half-oscillations per hour, whiplash precision index adjuster

**power reserve:** 45 hours after fully wound

**functions:** time display with hour, minutes and small seconds with seconds stop; moon phase display

**controls:** crown for winding the watch and for adjusting time, moon correction at ten o'clock

**case dimensions:** diameter 37.4 mm; height 8.9 mm

**glass and glass base:** anti-glare sapphire glass (hardness 9)

**watch movement dimensions:** diameter 27.5 mm; height 3.9 mm

**case:** honey-colored gold

**dial:** solid gold, argenté, guilloché; moon disc from solid honey-colored gold

**hands:** blued steel

**watch strap:** hand-sewn red-brown croco band with solid Lange pin buckle in honey-colored gold

**limitation:** 265 units

## 25. DATA SHEET LANGE 1 "LUMINOUS"

**watch movement:** Lange manufacture caliber L901.0, manual winding, created following the highest Lange quality criteria and assembled and decorated by hand; finely adjusted in five positions; double barrel; plates and bridges from natural nickel silver; hand-engraved balance cock

**parts watch movement:** 365

**bearing jewels:** 53; screwed gold chatons: 9

**escapement:** anchor escapement

**oscillation system** shock-proof glucydur screw balance, Nivarox spring, oscillating frequency of 21,600 half-oscillations per hour, whiplash precision index adjuster and patented drop-off adjustment

**power reserve:** time display with hour, minutes, small seconds with seconds stop, patented large date, power reserve indicator

**controls:** crown for winding the watch and adjusting time, date correction button

**case dimensions:** diameter 38.5 mm; height 10 mm; 18-carat white gold

**glass and glass base:** anti-glare sapphire glass (hardness 9)

**watch movement dimensions:** diameter 30,4 mm; height 5,9 mm

**dial:** solid silver, argenté; rhodium-plated gold appliqués, noctilucent

**hands:** rhodium-plated gold, noctilucent

**watch strap:** hand-sewn croco band with solid Lange pin buckle in solid white gold

## 26. DATA SHEET LANGE ZEITWERK "STRIKING TIME"

**watch movement:** Lange manufacture caliber L043.2, manual winding, created following the highest Lange quality criteria and assembled and decorated by hand; finely adjusted in five positions; three-quarter plate from natural nickel silver; hand-engraved balance cock; jumping minutes; continuous impulse via constant-force escapement

**parts watch movement:** 528

**bearing jewels:** 78; screwed gold chatons: 3

**escapement:** anchor escapement

**oscillation system** shock-proof glucydur balance with eccentric adjustment; balance spring of highest quality manufactured in-house with patented mounting (spiral clamp), oscillating frequency of 18,000 half-oscillations per hour, fine adjustment of drop-off with lateral adjustment screw and whiplash spring

**power reserve:** 36 hours when fully wound

**functions:** time display with hour and minutes as jumping display, small seconds with seconds stop, power reserve indicator, acoustic signal every quarter and full hour

**controls:** crown for winding the watch and for adjusting time; button to engage and disengage the acoustic signal

**case dimensions:** diameter 44.2 mm; height 13.1 mm

**glass and glass base:** anti-glare sapphire glass (hardness 9)

**watch movement dimensions:** diameter 36.0 mm; height 10.0 mm

**references:** 145.029, 145.025

**limitation:** none, in platinum: 100 units

**case:** white gold, platinum

**dial:** solid silver, black solid silver, with time bridge in nickel silver, rhodium-plated

**hands:** rhodium-plated gold

**watch strap:** hand-sewn croco band, black clasp: solid Lange pin buckle in white gold or solid Lange pin buckle in platinum

# 27. DATA SHEET RICHARD LANGE TOURBILLON "POUR LE MÉRITE"

**watch movement:** Lange manufacture caliber L072.1, manual winding, impulse via fusee and chain; created following the highest Lange quality criteria and assembled and decorated by hand; finely adjusted in five positions; three-quarter plate from natural nickel silver; hand-engraved seconds bridge

**parts watch movement:** 351 (without chain); parts chain: 636

**bearing jewels:** 32, one diamond endstone; screwed gold chatons: 3

**escapement:** anchor escapement

**oscillation system** shock-proof glucydur screw balance, balance spiral of highest quality manufactured in-house, oscillating frequency of 21,600 half-oscillations per hour

**power reserve:** 36 hours after fully wound

**functions:** time display with hour, minutes, small seconds; mintues tourbillon with patented seconds stop; pivoting dial

**controls:** crown for winding the watch and for adjusting time

**case dimensions:** diameter 41.9 mm; height 12.2 mm

**watch movement dimensions:** diameter 33.6 mm; height 7.6 mm

**references:** 760.032, 760.025

**limitation:** none, in platinum: 100 units

**case:** red gold, platinum

**dial:** solid silver, solid argenté silver, rhodié, hands red gold, rhodium-plated

**watch strap:** hand-sewn croco band, red-brown or hand-sewn croco band, black clasp: solid Lange folding clasp in red gold or solid Lange folding clasp in platinum

# 28. DATA SHEET SAXONIA DUAL TIME

**watch movement:** Lange manufacture caliber L086.2, automatic winding, created following the highest Lange quality criteria and assembled and decorated by hand; finely adjusted in five positions; plates from natural nickel silver; hand-engraved balance cock

**parts watch movement:** 268

**bearing jewels:** 31

**escapement:** anchor escapement

**oscillation system** shock-proof glucydur screw balance; balance spring of highest quality manufactured in-house, oscillating frequency of 21,600 half oscillations per hour, fine adjustment of the drop-off with lateral adjustment screw and whiplash spring

**power reserve:** 72 hours after fully wound

**functions:** time display with hour and

minutes, small seconds with seconds stop; display of a second time zone with second hour hand, 24-hour and day/night indicator

**controls:** crown for winding the watch and adjusting time; one button each for advancing and downshifting the time in steps of one hour

**case dimensions:** diameter 40.0 mm; height 9.1 mm

**watch movement dimensions:** diameter 30.4 mm; height 4.6 mm

**references:** 385.026, 385.032

**case:** white gold or red gold

**glass and glass base:** anti-glare sapphire glass (hardness 9)

**dial:** solid silver, solid argenté silver, argenté, gold hands, rhodium-plated; hour hands of the second time zone and 24-hour display blued steel; red gold

**watch strap:** hand-sewn croco band, black, or hand-sewn croco band, red-brown

**buckle:** solid Lange pin buckle in white gold or solid Lange pin buckle in red gold

## 29. DATA SHEET LANGE ZEITWERK "LUMINOUS"

**watch movement:** Lange manufacture caliber L043.1, manual winding, created following the highest Lange quality criteria and assembled and decorated by hand; finely adjusted in five positions; three-quarter plate from natural nickel silver; hand-engraved balance cock; jumping minutes; constant impulse via constant-force escapement

**parts watch movement:** 388

**bearing jewels:** 68; screwed gold chatons: 2

**escapement:** anchor escapement

**oscillation system** shock-proof glucydur balance with eccentric adjustments; balance spring of highest quality manufactured in-house with patented mounting (spiral clamp), oscillating frequency of 18,000 half-oscillations per hour, fine adjustment of the drop-off via lateral adjustment and whiplash spring

**power reserve:** 36 hours when fully wound

**functions:** time display with hour and minutes as jumping numerals, small seconds with seconds stop, power reserve indicator

**controls:** crown for winding up the watch and for adjusting the time

**case dimensions:** diameter 41.9 mm; height 12.6 mm

**watch movement dimensions:** diameter 33.6 mm; height 9.3 mm

**references:** 140.035

**case:** platinum

**glass and glass base:** anti-glare sapphire glass (hardness 9) dial: sapphire glass, coated; noctilucent numerals, time bridge nickel silver, PVD- coated

hands: rhodium-plated gold

watch strap: hand-sewn croco band, black

buckle: solid Lange pin buckle in platinum

limitation: 100 units

## 30. DATA SHEET SAXONIA "THIN"

watch movement: Lange manufacture caliber L093.1, manual winding, created following the highest Lange quality criteria and assembled and decorated by hand; finely adjusted in five positions; plates from natural nickel silver; hand-engraved balance cock

parts watch movement: 167

bearing jewels: 21; screwed gold chatons: 3

escapement: anchor escapement

oscillation system shock-proof glucydur screw balance; balance spring of highest quality manufactured in-house, oscillating frequency of 21,600 half-oscillations per hour

power reserve: 72 hours after fully wound

funcrtions: time display with hour and minutes

controls: crown for winding the watch and for adjusting time

case dimensions: diameter 40.0 mm; height 5.9 mm

watch movement dimensions: diameter 28 mm; height 2.9 mm

case: red gold

glass and glass base: sapphire glass (hardness 9)

## 31. DATA SHEET CABARET

watch movement: Lange manufacture caliber L.931.3, manual winding, created following the highest Lange quality criteria and assembled and decorated by hand; finely adjusted in five positions; plates and bridges from natural cross-rolled nickel silver; hand-engraved balance cock

parts watch movement: 237

bearing jewels: 31, screwed gold chatons: 3

escapement: anchor escapement

oscillation system shock-proof glucydur screw balance, Nivarox 1 spring with an oscillating frequency of 21,600 half-oscillations per hour, whiplash precison index adjuster and patented drop-off adjustment

power reserve: 42 hours when fully wound

functions: hour, minutes, small seconds with seconds stop, patented large date

controls: crown for winding the watch and adjusting time, a button recessed into the case for adjusting the large date case: 36.3 x 25.5 mm, yellow, white, red gold, and platinum

glass and glass base: sapphire glass (hardness 9)

dials: solid silver in champagne or argenté and black; gold appliqués

hands: yellow or red gold and white gold

watch straps: hand-sewn croco bands, solid Lange pin buckle in gold

## 32. DATA SHEET DATOGRAPH AUF/AB

watch movement: Lange manufacture caliber L951.6, manual winding, created following the highest Lange quality criteria and assembled and decorated by hand; finely adjusted in five positions; plates and bridges from natural nickel silver; hand-engraved balance cock

parts watch movement: 451

bearing jewels: 46, screwed gold chatons: 4

escapement: anchor escapement

oscillation system shock-proof balance with eccentric adjustments; balance spring of highest quality manufactured in-house, oscillating frequency of 18,000 half-oscillations per hour, fine adjustment of the drop-off with lateral adjustment screw and whiplash spring

power reserve: 60 hours when fully wound

functions: time display with hour, minutes and small seconds with seconds stop; flyback chronograph with precise jumping minutes counter; power reserve display; large date

controls: crown for winding up the watch and adjusting the time, two buttons for controlling the chronograph, one button for quick correction of the large date

case dimensions: diameter: 41.0 mm; height: 13.1 mm

watch movement dimensions: diameter: 30.6 mm; height: 7.9 mm

case: platinum; glass and glass base: sapphire glass (hardness 9)

dial: solid silver, black

hands: rhodium-plated gold; steel

watch strap: hand-sewn croco band, blue-grey

buckle: Lange pin buckle in platinum

# Further Reading

Braun, Peter (Hrsg.): *A. Lange & Söhne. Geschichte, Design, Techik (A. Lange & Söhne. History, Design, Technology)*, Heel Verlag, Königswinter 2003

Dittrich, Herbert: *Die Messung des Augenblicks. Wie die genaue Zeit nach Glashütte kam (The Measurement of the Moment. How Precise Time came to Glashütte)*, Sandstein Verlag, Dresden 2008

Dittrich, Herbert: *Der Beginn einer Tradition. Die ersten 50 Jahre der Präzisionsuhren-Herstellung in Glashütte von 1845 bis 1895 (The Beginning of a Tradition. The First 50 Years of Precision Watchmaking in Glashütte from 1845 to 1895)*, Sandstein Verlag, Dresden 2009

Dittrich, Herbert: *Erfinder und Visionäre. Die Erfinder der Präzisionsuhren-Herstellung in Dresden und Glashütte (Inventors and Visionaries. The Inventors of Precision Watchmaking in Dresden and Glashütte)*, Sandstein Verlag, Dresden 2009

Dittrich, Herbert: *Die Kunst der Genauigkeit. Die Wurzeln der Präzisionsuhren-Herstellung in Sachsen (The Art of Precision. The Roots of Precision Watchmaking in Saxony)*, Sandstein Verlag, Dresden 2009

Herkner, Kurt: *Glashütte und seine Uhren (Glashütte and its Watches)*, Herkner-Verlag, Dormagen, 1. Auflage 1978, 2. überarbeitete Auflage 1988

Herkner, Kurt: *Glashütter Armbanduhren von der ersten Fertigung bis zur Gegenwart. Die Weiterentwicklung der Unternehmen nach 1945 (Glashütte Wristwatches from the Beginning to the Present. The Development of the Company after 1945)*, Herkner-Verlag, Dormagen, 1. Auflage 1994

Huber, Martin: *Die Uhren von A. Lange & Söhne, Glashütte/Sachsen (The Watches of A. Lange & Söhne, Glashütte/Saxony)*, Callwey-Verlag, Munich, 1. Auflage 1977, 6. Auflage 1997

Huber, Martin: *Die Lange Liste: Die Werknummern der komplizierten Taschenuhren und Armbanduhren von A. Lange & Söhne, Glashütte, von 1845–1945 (The Lange List: the movement numbers of the complicated pocket watches and writstwatches by A. Lange & Söhne, Glashütte, from 1845–1945)*, (Ergänzungsband zu Huber 1977), Munich 2000

Kreuzer, Anton: *Die Armbanduhr. Geschichte, Technik, Design (The Wristwatch. History, Technology, Design)*, Carinthia Verlag, Klagenfurt 1995

Lange, Walter: *Als die Zeit nach Hause kam. Erinnerungen (When Time Came Home)*, Econ Verlag, Berlin 2004

Meis, Reinhard: *A. Lange & Söhne – Eine Uhrmacher-Dynastie aus Dresden (A. Lange & Sons - A Watchmaker Dynasty from Dresden)*, Callwey-Verlag, München, 2. Auflage 1999

Meis, Reinhard: *A. Lange & Söhne – The Watchmakers of Dresden*, Antiquorum Editions, Genf 1999